An Atmospherics of the City

VERBAL ARTS :: STUDIES IN POETICS

SERIES EDITORS :: Lazar Fleishman and Haun Saussy

ROSS CHAMBERS

An Atmospherics of the City

Baudelaire and the Poetics of Noise

Fordham University Press

New York 2015

Fordham University Press also publishes its books in a variety of electronic formats. Some content that appears in print may not be available in electronic books.

Visit us online at www.fordhampress.com.

Library of Congress Cataloging-in-Publication Data available online at catalog.loc.gov.

Printed in the United States of America

17 16 15   5 4 3 2 1

First edition

This essay is dedicated

to the memory

of Helen Tartar.

CONTENTS

PREFACE

The initial impetus for this essay lay in an invitation from the Department of French at the University of California, Berkeley, to give a series of seminars, of which the outlines can be read in my chapters. For their very great kindness and warm welcome, my sincere thanks go to the faculty, the staff, and the students of the Berkeley department. For their exceptional kindness and hospitality, as well as for the encouragement and intellectual stimulus their own work has provided me over many years, I owe a special debt to Michael Lucey, Debarati Sanyal, and Ann Smock.

The question underlying the Berkeley seminars was that of the uncanny "supernaturalism" that Baudelaire always seems to have understood as a crucial component of modern poetic beauty. What became of the Romantic sublime when, instead of inhabiting the countryside as Wordsworth did, poets came to live in the crowded, grimy, and usually insalubrious streets of the new cities that arose following, and as a consequence of, the Industrial Revolution?

In France, the major writers of Baudelaire's generation—Nerval, Gautier, Flaubert—seem to have subscribed to a practice of fetishizing beauty—one not structurally different from the commodity fetishism that Marx was later to describe. Baudelaire too was a skilled practitioner of this mode of poetic artifice, and seems never to have repudiated it. But "dépolitiqué" (as he famously put it)—cleansed of the utopian political aspirations of the 1840s by the disastrous events of 1848–51 and the installation of the Second Empire—Baudelaire's worldview became a more deeply pessimistic one.

A new urban supernaturalism entailed a reading of the atmospherics of the city as a shroud that partly concealed and partly revealed a divine but malevolent principle of sinister activity—what would now be called *entropy*—that he viewed as governing human history and making it a temporal phenomenon of endless decline. Imagined as a kind of city weather made of the background noise of urban life, it is this weather of time that is now identifiable as the form of supernaturalism at work in the great allegorical poems of the second (1861) edition of *Les Fleurs du Mal.* Tugging at the reader's sleeve like a prostitute or a beggar, or striking like a thunderbolt in the glance of an elegant passerby, the poems seek readerly attention with a view to producing a necessary disalienation. And in the prose poems of *Le Spleen de Paris,* the noise of city life ironically invades the collection itself, which—in the guise of the poet's "urban diary"—bears witness to the power of entropy in its own inability to take definitive shape or to conclude.

In this way, I suggest, the supernaturalism of the sublime, in becoming poetry of the subliminal presence of noise, gives rise, in passing through the medium of Baudelaire's historical pessimism, to a poetics of modernity that might be defined as poetry's recognition of that which is most inimical to the poetic urge. In incorporating into poetry, as he did, that which could only be regarded as fundamentally alien to the poetic urge, Baudelaire introduced a new, modern form of beauty, and a new function of the aesthetic: a poetics of poetry's other, its enemy; one that is informed by an exigency of veracity and motivated by the desire to bear historical witness.

I also want to thank Neil Doshi, Matthieu Dupas, and Mélissa Gélinas for their work at the computer; and special thanks go to David Caron for his trust and encouragement.

In what follows I supply translations into English of French words and phrases, as well as of quotations from Baudelaire's essays, personal jottings, and prose poems. Translations of verse poems are those of Richard Howard in Charles Baudelaire, *Les Fleurs du Mal* (Boston, MA: David R. Godine, 1982). In discussions of prosodic detail I cite the French text only, as also on occasions where meaning is supplied by the context. With the exception of "Les sept vieillards" and "Le Cygne," which are included with their translation in the appendix, verse poems that are the object of extended discussion are cited and translated in the text. The abbreviations *OC* and *C* refer to the Pléiade editions of Baudelaire's *Œuvres complètes* and *Correspondance* respectively, and will be accompanied by volume and page numbers.

Das bekannte überhaupt ist darum, weil es bekannt ist, nicht erkannt.

G. W. F. Hegel, *Phänomenologie des Geistes*

Soulagement et gloire uniques,
—La conscience dans le Mal!

Baudelaire, "L'Irrémédiable"

La vie parisienne est féconde en sujets poétiques et merveilleux. Le merveilleux nous enveloppe et nous abreuve comme l'atmosphère; mais nous ne le voyons pas.

Baudelaire, *Salon de 1846*

Deux qualités littéraires fondamentales: surnaturalisme et ironie.

Baudelaire, *Fusées III* (1855–62)

The familiar, for the very reason that it is familiar, cannot be known.

G. W. F. Hegel, *Phenomenology of Spirit*

Our only relief and glory,
—Awareness within Evil!

Baudelaire, "The Irremediable"

Parisian life is fertile in poetic and wondrous subjects. The wondrous enwraps us and slakes our thirst like the atmosphere; but we fail to see it.

Baudelaire, *The Salon of 1846*

Two fundamental literary qualities: supernaturalism and irony.

Baudelaire, *Rockets III* (1855–62)

PART I

Fetish and the Everyday

ONE

From the Sublime to the Subliminal: Fetish Aesthetics

Mobilized Attention

How to define an atmosphere? The word has a specific primary sense, of course, and a scientific definition. It is the invisible layer of breathable air that swathes the planet, sustaining life and exerting the variable pressure we register as weather. Weather is not irrelevant to a poetics of urban atmosphere. But to speak of the atmospherics of a city is also to activate a derived sense of the word, one in which *atmosphere* refers to the intuition one has, or rather the subliminal awareness, of a certain dimension of particularity, otherness, or strangeness that attaches to certain objects, places, or situations that in other respects are recognizable as ordinary, familiar, or not worthy of special attention. To become aware of an atmosphere—and one of Baudelaire's most important understandings of poetry is as an agent of such a becoming aware—is to become bafflingly conscious of something that one had been already aware of, somehow, but without knowing it. This is the sense of there being an ungraspable or even uncanny hinterland of things, a dimension that defies definition or analysis because it lies just beyond the domain of the intelligible, and endows them with a mysterious significance. Something like what we refer to when we speak of a city having "local color."

Fetish objects, in particular, are ordinary things that have been strangely "promoted" in this way: an item of clothing, perhaps; or an object on display in a store; or some ugly-looking figurine that "buzzes" you when you approach it in an anthropological museum. Such objects have or have acquired an atmosphere—a fact that perhaps suggests that the word *atmosphere* is associated with the sublimation of desire that is at the root of fetish theory, and hence, ultimately, with forms of beauty and of the sacred. I am not far from saying, in fact, that they are or have become *allegorized*; and by that I mean that if they "speak" to us, it is to bespeak "otherness."[1] And that is why this phenomenon—whereby the familiar trappings of everyday existence, those that we normally pay little or no attention to, become strange and somehow alien when, for whatever reason, we are led to *notice* them, to attend to their existence and their presence—might be thought of as an effect of aesthetic fetishization. Independently of (specifically) erotic, consumerist, or religious desire, attention and the framing of an object that it requires activate in us a need for meaningfulness, and do so to the exact degree that the object has been previously perceived—or rather not perceived at all—as trivial. In becoming thus allegorized, the object then activates a *libido intelligendi*, a desire to understand, the strength of which is doubtless a function of the Weberian "disenchantment" to which the modern world seems increasingly subject, since it is the unexpected perception of the everyday world as strange that activates it. Whence that frustrating, tip-of-the-tongue sense of a just-out-of-reach "meaning" that constitutes an atmospherics.

That Baudelaire was a prime mover in insisting on the indispensable role of the category of the aesthetic in the modern age is not a matter of dispute. My contention will be that it was in defining the practice of modern art as an atmospherics of urban life, and in practicing such an atmospherics as an allegorization of a *vie parisienne* that had become everyday reality for his readers, that he invented a new (or rather previously unacknowledged) function for the category of the aesthetic amid the utilitarianism of bourgeois modernity. Art, as a practice of atmospherics, was to enact something like the etymological sense of the word *aesthetics*; poetry as he practiced it was to function as an *aesthesis* capable of *making sensible* the dimension of strangeness inherent, most notably, in the "moving chaos" of the familiar urban street.[2] It would be a way of channeling the "wonder" that "swathes and nourishes us like the atmosphere" but, in the absence of artistic intervention, remains invisible and goes unheeded. Art was to function, in other words, as an antianaesthetics, deploying poiesis as a practice of *making* capable of transfiguring the ordinary, the unremarkable, the ugly, and the apparently unredeemable because utilitarian, and thus—if not of reenchanting a world bereft of mystery and glamour—then at least of awakening the poet's readers to the unconscious state of alienation in which they lived. (I employ the Marxian word unapologetically.[3])

As early as the *Salon de 1846*, then, *atmosphère* was already a key term of Baudelairean aesthetics. Painting is superior to sculpture, he claims there, with his usual imperturbable assurance (and reserving as always his "droit de se contredire" [right to self-contradiction]), and this is because the atmosphere of a painting—conveyed, in technical terms by its form, its particular deployment of color and light—can be taken in at a glance, and as it were, subconsciously. Statues, on the other hand, are too much like natural objects, which are only *environnés d'atmosphère* (surrounded by atmosphere) and, for that very reason, require a more exploratory and analytical approach, one that needs time in order to take in their spatial dimensions—something that Baudelaire judges to be "primitive" by comparison with the magical immediacy of painting's directness. They are, in the only sense of the word Baudelaire recognized, "fetishes" (and sculpture, therefore is *ennuyeuse* [tedious, annoying]).[4] The irony is of course that the inventor of modern art should not be able, in 1846, to foresee the enthusiasm for African and Oceanic masks and fetish objects that was to sweep the "capital of the nineteenth century" in the early years of the twentieth century and would signal a contribution to the invention of modernism. Nevertheless, Baudelaire's invocation of atmosphere defined the very principle of that new aesthetics; and it will be important for us, therefore, to attend to his later, radically revised, judgment with respect to sculpture as I approach allegory in its relation to "fetish aesthetics" in chapter 3.

Meanwhile, recalling M. H. Abrams's famous characterization of the aesthetics of the sublime as "natural supernaturalism," we might think of Baudelairean atmospherics as an urban, or artificial, supernaturalism—perhaps even a "subliminalism."[5] For the Romantic cult of the sublime appears as the principal forerunner of the mid-century turn away from Romanticism that I am interested in—the turn to an art of fetish-like "atmosphere" held to define "modern beauty," and doing so in terms of a *merveilleux* detectable in the everyday world of urban modernity. This latter moment thus appears as a further stage, following the era of the sublime, in the Enlightenment and post-Enlightenment history of the de-sacralization of art—a history that itself arises as an entailment of the aesthetic function's newly acquired status as an agent of the reenchantment of the world. Turning away from the noble and stirring spectacles of nature that reveal themselves at the *limen* or threshold, connecting but separating the immanent world and the transcendence of the sacred, a new generation now looks for inspiration to an apparently barren cultural scene of manufacture, production, and trade. But there it discovers two things.

One of those things is the subliminality (if not the sublimity) of a simultaneously conscious and unconscious experience, the becoming aware of that of which one had been unaware. This is an experience not unlike that of the uncanny, but it resembles in its strangeness the Marxian experience of disalienation and is described by Baudelaire in terms of the city's atmosphere. Such an awareness of the uncanny has historical roots, of course, in the aesthetics of the gothic and the fantastic, with their emphasis on mysterious intimations of a beyond. But the other discovery is that of the power of artistic shaping: of *form* and the labor of *mise en forme*. It is form that molds an object of representation, and by isolating and framing it as an object of attention reawakens in the observer a sense of wonderment and desire, an awareness of atmosphere, in the presence of something otherwise recognizable as familiar and ordinary—the very sense, that is, that the dailiness of city life tends to erode. In Marx's analysis of commodity fetishism, it is labor that transforms an object having only use value into one that enjoys the added attractiveness he calls exchange value. But the condition of such a transformation is that the crucial input of labor must be rendered transparent, and thus invisible. Similarly, artistic form, the mark of aesthetic labor, can reveal the atmospherics of its object as a practice of beautification and agency of wonder, but only under the condition of becoming itself invisible. Such is the shamanistic sleight-of-hand of a fetishizing aesthetics—a magic that Baudelaire initially subscribed to, but in the end, came to challenge, as we shall see.[6]

Awakening to Noise

That challenge arose as a consequence of a lifelong evolution in the poet's assessment of the value and significance of noise—of noise as an inevitable component of an aesthetics of fetish he had initially conceived as the necessary harmonizing of noisy everyday ugliness associated with city life, and the intimations of a timeless, ideal beauty, the sublimity that nature was held to offer. This essay offers a review of the evidence available to us in Baudelaire's poetic writing of that extended and painful evolution, which itself manifestly occurred in response to the major social upheavals France was undergoing in his (short) lifetime. I mean on the one hand the brutal transition, if *transition* is the word, from a largely rural society to one dominated by a new industrial, urban, and capitalist economy increasingly devoted to bourgeois values—in other words, the traumatic coming of modernity—and on the other hand the political violence and other upheavals, most notably of the post-1848 period, that made the enthusiastic early socialist and harmonian dreams of the 1830s and 1840s seem like so many naïve and irresponsible fantasies. My outline of Baudelaire's evolution will tell not only a story of disillusionment, but also of remarkable intellectual and aesthetic flexibility and adaptability. And although I will have to present it methodically, as if it were a straightforward and unidirectional movement forward, it will be worth remembering that while Baudelaire displays an astonishing thirst for new thought and fresh ideas, changing his mind with alacrity, he also seems never to have fully abandoned any aesthetic conviction he once held, even as he kept moving on, new experiment by new experiment. (Whence, of course, his ardent if ironic defense of "le droit de se contredire.") After all, the inventor of "modern beauty," it should be remembered, was simultaneously among the last of France's most classical poets: an inspiration to Rimbaud and, later, the Surrealists while admired and appreciated by the Parnassians. The story of his awakening to noise, then, was itself inevitably a noisy one, as indeed are most evolutions, although my brief essay cannot help but simplify and schematize it.

Given Baudelaire's interest in atmosphere, a confrontation with noise was inevitable, if only because noise, in all of the word's many possible senses, was and is the crucial constituent of any modern city's atmospherics. Noise is both the deafening racket one cannot ignore—the "rue assourdissante" (deafening street) of "À une passante"—and the largely unnoticed, because persistent and familiar, background to city dwellers' lives: that of which we become conscious only to realize that we had always been, in some sense, aware of it, without having known that we were (something that "Les sept vieillards" might be thought to allegorize). Both alienating and disalienating in this sense, noise is also a convenient metaphor for the many forms of disorder, disarray, distraction, and fragmented experience offered by the life of the street, like the "chaos mouvant" (moving chaos) of traffic—in Baudelaire's day not yet regulated—so compellingly described in "Perte d'auréole," or of course the innumerable busy *chantiers*, the messy worksites that disrupted the cityscape in the Haussmann era, as described in "Le Cygne" and represented in the extraordinary lithographs and photographs of the period (e.g., Daumier and Marville).[7]

Finally, the word *noise* today designates all the static or interference that arises in channels of communication, and by extension the entropy that similarly affects all functioning systems and makes their smoothest operations secretly inefficient, a parasitic presence that is both necessary to life and the consumer of our energy and being. The laws of thermodynamics that include and enshrine the concept of entropy were formulated early in the nineteenth century as a direct consequence of the Industrial Revolution and the invention of the steam engine; but Baudelaire seems unaware of this sense of the word *noise.* He does, however, recognize the phenomenon itself—in the disorderly energy, the "electricity" of the crowd, for instance, and in the alienated encounters, the failures to connect, that are dramatized in so many of the prose poems in *Le Spleen de Paris.* So finally we might recognize the devastating whistle that fatally interrupts the mime's entrancing performance in "Une mort héroïque" as the poet's most striking representation of noise's destructive power, as well as of its direct relevance to art.

And if Baudelaire connects noise in all its possible senses to the brooding atmosphere that enshrouds the city of Paris, it is because, finally, he intuits its relation, not only to the pressure of weather with its threatening storms—*le temps qu'il fait*—but also to the passing of time, as well as the destructive force of devastating events and violent change that are sometimes generated out of the unheeded, moment-by-moment, temporal process and recognized as history: *le temps qui passe.* Tellingly, the noisy street, where one is exposed to weather and to passing time, is for Baudelaire both the site where the city's atmosphere is most readily detected and the site where history happens. And that is doubtless why the many permanent denizens of the street—I mean those who eke out some kind of existence there and themselves form a crucial part of its noisy life—seem to be endowed with a special knowledge that escapes the busy passers-by who hurry from point *A* to point *B.* The ragpickers, beggars, prostitutes, and street performers of all kinds (mimes, *saltimbanques,* musicians)—the whole class of *forains,* those "on the outside" (Latin *foris*)—both attract and intrigue the flâneur poet, himself an habitué of the street. They do so, I suggest, because on the one hand they form part of the city's atmosphere, personifying its noisy life in their fringe existence, while on the other they appear to have acquired a wisdom from their exposed existence that indoor dwellers—a metaphor for the *bourgeoisie*—are unaware of. "Les Yeux des pauvres" is readable, perhaps, as an allegory of this tantalizing (un)readability of Baudelaire's street people.[8]

All this city noise—alienating din, steady background hum, unruly disorder bordering on chaos but also a certain intriguing strangeness—contrasts, of course, with the supposed stillness, silence, and timelessness of "immutable" nature. (That nature is itself subject to entropy is a post-Baudelairean realization.) Baudelaire's awakening to noise as the specific indicator of urban modernity and the crucial component of the city's atmosphere is interestingly literalized in a recent novel by the Australian writer Gail Jones. *Dreams of Speaking*—a title that resonates with Baudelaire's own pursuit of a language of noise—is an "Alice in Wonderland" novel, one that epitomizes our inheritance of a post-Baudelairean aesthetics of modernity as the sense of strange and indeed alien beauty associated with, specifically, urban civilization. It entwines the twin themes of disenchanted reenchantment—the unsuspected strangeness of the familiar and the similarly unnoticed noisiness of the world—in an exploration of the atmospherics of cities (Perth, Australia; Paris; Nagasaki, Japan), a poetics of technological gadgetry (interestingly akin to Baudelaire's "Morale du joujou" [1853]), and finally an account of the strains and pleasures of alienated relations (an irritatingly persistent ex-boyfriend; the comfortable friendship of a young Australian woman with an elderly Japanese survivor of Hiroshima; the *un*comfortable loving affections of an adopted daughter and her therefore unrelated parents and sister). Still jet-lagged from her long flight from

Australia, Alice awakens in the night in her Paris apartment in the Marais, near the Seine:

> In the middle of the night she heard it again—the sound of the river. Then she listened carefully and once more found that she was mistaken. What she heard this time was the material commotion of the city: sirens, wheels, decelerating buses, footsteps, calls, mobile phones. There was the squeal of an almost collision and a cry of abuse. There was a plane overhead, dragging decibels in its wake. Vehicles of every kind. The snarl of a motorbike. The rumble of garbage trucks with their brute growling innards, the roll and click-clack of a late-night skateboard. All this activity in the air, this routine distortion. All this noisy encasement and mobilized intention. Alice wanted silence. She wanted the nullity of deep space. In her bed in Paris, she experienced a twinge of homesickness. Not the longing for a place, so much, as for a space into which her self could be poured, without erasure.[9]

Alice's middle-of-the night awakening to noise has been carefully naturalized. Accustomed to the relative silence of her Perth neighborhood, she may find Paris's brand of nocturnal noise especially disturbing; perhaps too she mistakes the "material commotion of the city" for the sound of the nearby Seine, because in Perth she lives near the Swan and windsurfs on its estuary-like bays. In her sleepy wakefulness, the two cities are unconsciously melded: one a lost space of heedless comfort "into which her self could be poured, without erasure," the other one that threatens to "erase" that sense of self. The latter is the double space of disalienation, of awakening accompanied by a nostalgia for the alienated unawareness that preceded this new state of disorientation. In Baudelaire, we shall find something quite similar.[10]

Alice's new alertness to "this activity in the air, this routine distortion" that constitutes the atmospherics of Paris is

Baudelaire-like too in its pairing of "material commotion" with "mobilized intention," a phrase that refers, I take it, to the purposefulness of street traffic in all its decibel-laden vehicular variety, from planes overhead to skateboards, but which also suggests the *intentness* of Alice's own awakened attention: her mobilized *noticing* of a commotion that by day had seemingly gone unheeded. It is as if the threat represented by the now-awakened awareness of noise as entropy, the danger of erosion and eventual erasure that means the death of the self, is balanced by a negentropic counterintentness, as if the value of the mobilized awareness compensated for the energy lost unconsciously to noise. Lucidity, or—as he puts it in his own-terms "la conscience dans le Mal"—is surely for Baudelaire not only the supreme virtue to which modern man can aspire but perhaps also the only value to which one can aspire (see "L'Irrémédiable," poem 84 of *Les Fleurs du Mal*).

Such lucid attention is what the passage suggests, on Alice's part, in its deployment of the wealth of words that the lexicon of English makes available, its frequently onomatopoeic registration in language of noise's variety as well as its constant presence. It is as if language itself offers evidence of a widely shared noise anxiety, like Alice's and Baudelaire's, that may not often surface in the way it does here but is active in the linguistic unconscious and offers the detached observer a means of exploration and analysis in the way that Inuit languages are fabled for their complex terminology of snow. And if, as I am suggesting, noise anxiety is akin to, or even a version of, time anxiety—our simultaneous denial and unconsciousness of time's erosion (but also unending renewal) of life—there is another Baudelairean aspect to this passage, one on which I want to expand a little. It is, of course, the equivalence of streets and rivers.

This is the second time Alice has been awakened by the river, only to realize that what she was hearing was traffic noise. But the first time her attention had stayed focused on the noise's riverine quality: perhaps, she had reflected, it was the "idea of the river that seemed somehow audible." What this means is hinted at when she goes on to evoke the "mystery of nature": "Energies beyond machines. Beyond petrochemical drive." This riverine "idea" in Alice's understanding, is something antecedent to modernity, then, with its traffic and the Xerox-machine to whose sound she had originally compared the "rhythmic, thunderous sound" of the Seine—the Seine which itself, when she had first seen it, had likewise impressed her with the antiquity of its own "venerable, khaki-coloured" rift, "older than Europe" or if you will its own premodern "idea." Baudelaire's (necessarily pre-Xerox) figure for this same riverine ideality—the ancient, obstinate, rhythmic noise attributed to the drift of time—is the autumnal thud of logs being unloaded in a courtyard, as in "Chant d'automne" (poem 57): "J'entends déjà tomber avec des chocs funèbres / Le bois retentissant sur le pavé des cours" (I hear them chopping firewood in our court / the dreary thud of logs on cobblestone). But in Baudelaire this funereal sound has no apparent connection with the drifting flow of rivers: the Parisian poetic tradition Alice's apprehension of the Seine indexes is, of course, *not* that of the mid-nineteenth century, but that of Apollinaire ("Sous le pont Mirabeau coule la Seine" [Below the Mirabeau Bridge flows the Seine]), and of Apollinaire-like successor poets such as Raymond Queneau and Jacques Roubaud.

As a poet of Paris, Baudelaire is of another era, then, and the Seine, perhaps surprisingly to modern readers, occupies an insignificant and well-nigh undetectable place in his vision of the city—the same being true, *mutatis mutandis,* not only of Balzac, his great predecessor, but also of his own contemporaries, Théophile Gautier and Gérard de Nerval. The Seine, to them, is not a factor. A hint as to why this is so is offered, however, by yet another member of Baudelaire's generation, Gustave Flaubert, in the memorable opening page of *L'Education sentimentale* in which Frédéric Moreau departs from Paris, amid much noise and bustle, aboard the paddleboat on which he is about to encounter for the first time Mme Arnoux. Until the spreading network of railroads gradually replaced them, rivers in France mainly functioned as thoroughfares, and were consequently associated with traffic, commerce, and industry. In Paris, the Seine was to all intents and purposes, a kind of city street, then—something that Flaubert broadly hints at by showing us the objects of Frédéric's attention as the boat moves upstream in the direction of Nogent. At first, warehouses, building sites, and factories "populate" the two banks; then, as the boat continues to move, the familiar urban tangle of Paris now disappears into the fog:

> A travers le brouillard [Frédéric] contemplait des clochers, des édifices dont il ne savait pas les noms; puis il embrassa, dans un dernier coup d'oeil, l'île Saint-Louis, la Cité, Notre-Dame; et bientôt, Paris disparaissant, il poussa un grand soupir.
>
> (Through the fog Frédéric watched the bell towers and buildings whose name he did not know; then in one final glance he took in the Île Saint-Louis, the Cité, and Notre-Dame, until soon, as Paris disappeared, he heaved a great sigh.)
>
> *L'Éducation sentimentale*, 1

This fog, picking up on the departure scene of frenzied activity whose noise (*tapage*) is absorbed into an all-enveloping whitish cloud of hissing steam, suggests that, in its own way, Flaubert's novel is defining itself, like Baudelaire's poetry, as an atmospherics of the city of Paris, and doing so in terms both industrial and meteorological.

Flaubert's "deux berges, peuplées de magasins, de chantiers et d'usines" (two riverbanks, crowded with shops, worksites, and factories)—located in the very heart of the city—also confirms the idea that rivers, including the Seine, are not so much absent from *Les Fleurs du Mal* as they have been subsumed into the city's streets, which—as themselves sites of drift and flow that make visible as well as audible the steady disorder of time's endless passing—function like rivers no longer natural but man-made, rivers that are the product of human artifice. If, as Heraclitus famously put it, no one steps twice into the same river, the same is true of streets, those noisy urbanized channels and arteries that are sites of pedestrian flow and vehicular chaos, and where also the city's atmosphere—readable in the eyes of the poor and the litter of seedy humanity with whom Baudelaire associates the poet and the work of poetry—becomes palpable in the electric energy of the crowd. But if, like rivers, streets make manifest the noisy process of passing-by that is the movement of duration, they differ from rivers in that, as sites of human life, they are also places where sometimes, out of the flux of process, an *event* can emerge. History can happen in the streets, whether it be in the form of the poet's strange encounters with spectral old men, stray swans, or elegant widows whose glance strikes like a hurricane—encounters that can lastingly change an individual's existence—or of the collective political uprisings whose memory still remains associated, in French, with the very word *rue* and the street's riotous, surging crowds: events that change the life of a society, and in Baudelaire's eyes, rarely if ever do so for the better.

For *descendre dans la rue* (to step into the street)—a phrase that refers both to an everyday action and to political recourse to *l'émeute*—is an act charged with symptomatic significance. The verb *descendre,* itself suggestive of decline, figures in the standard French version of Heraclitus's dictum: "On ne descend pas deux fois dans le même fleuve" (One does not step twice into the same river); but it also inscribes the *downward* direction that is as characteristic of Baudelairean *spleen* as upward movement is the marker of *l'idéal.* "Bientôt nous descendrons dans les froides ténèbres" (Soon we shall descend into the cold darkness) is the opening line of "Chant d'automne," and the steady rhythm of the woodblocks resounding "sur le pavé des cours" (on the cobblestones) is that, not only of autumn, but also of a funeral march. I will follow a similar downward movement, from a kind of pseudotranscendence to an ultimate embrace of immanence, as I trace the direction of Baudelaire's aesthetic evolution—an evolution simultaneously revolutionary and downward-turning, and thus twice inscribed in the street, as is *la beauté moderne* (modern beauty) itself in relation to *la beauté idéale* (ideal beauty) of the optimistic 1830s and 1840s (the concept to which Gautier, for instance, was to cling throughout his long life).[11] But finally, too, downward movement for Baudelaire—and increasingly so after the events of 1848–51—is the inevitable direction followed by human civilization itself; that is, the direction of a history of decline as opposed to nature's supposedly unchanging permanence. And the city street, where history happens, emerging out of process time in the way that the elegant widow of "À une passante" with her devastating glance emerges from the crowd, is thus, for the poet, the very sign of this inescapable decadence of human civilization, the evidence of our fallen state.

If Baudelaire's noise-filled streets are displaced rivers, then it is that very displacement that suggests their most crucial significance. The word *rue,* it is true, echoes an old word for stream (*un ru*) as well as the verb *ruer* (to rush), and this riverine echo resonates, for example, in "Les sept vieillards," where the fog transforms an ordinary street into a flooded river, a "rivière accrue." But in "Le Cygne," the "nouveau Carrousel" becomes a place of *memory*, where "ce petit fleuve, . . . Ce Simoïs menteur qui par vos pleurs grandit" (that . . . mimic Simoïs salted by your tears) bespeaks Andromache's fall, from the sublimity of the epic into the reality of historical time, and with it into the baseness of the trivial, the ordinary, and the everyday—the site both of deceitful artifice ("Simoïs *menteur*") and of what, punning on *la ville* (the city), Baudelaire had already identified, in "Le Soleil," as "le vil" (the vile). But these swollen rivers, too, are brimming, not only with the accumulation of historical time but also with the imminence of a more particular revelation: the spectral apparition of the ghostly old men, or the unexpected connection made in the poet's mind between ancient Andromache and the modern exile of the swan, stranded in the dust of an urban gutter, out of place and far from water of *any* kind, be it lake or river. So, it is finally the emergence of "la passante," she who passes by, out of "la rue assourdissante" (the deafening street) that represents the crucial instance of such a revelation, signifying as she does just such an emergence of the historical, in the form of a devastating event, out of the noisy crowd and the ongoing process of temporal drift, the time of the everyday. For such events are moments that bring a tantalizing sense of partial insight. As such they are not the concern of nature, although natural rivers too may flood. They are the product of human society, the *polis*: the city as *cité* as well as *ville*, the *civitas* that accompanies the *urbs*.

For where there is history, there is also—and necessarily so, as Walter Benjamin so fruitfully argued—allegory.[12] Allegory is a reflection on the ruins—the devastation, the dispersal, the noisy residue—that are themselves a seemingly interpretable remainder, partly of time per se, but also of history's destructive power. If Baudelaire's streets, in their guise of "fallen" rivers, are swollen with imminent revelation, then—a form of readability—it is not that they promise access to actual knowledge. It is rather that humanity's fall into history permits only the kind of frustrated recognition of our nonknowledge that composes the significance of allegorical thought. The word for such a recognition, which one might think of as the wisdom of the street, is, I suggest, *disalienation*—that is, the *recognition of human alienation,* something that is not the same as becoming in some miraculous way *un*alienated. Allegory, then, can and does dispel illusion, but it does so, as we shall see at greater length, without installing in its place the possibility of knowing. As in "À une passante," it is exactly the figure of a missed encounter with actual knowledge, a *rencontre manquée*:

> Car j'ignore où tu fuis, tu ne sais où je vais,
> O toi que j'eusse aimée, ô toi qui le savais!
>
> (Of me you know nothing, I nothing of you
> whom I might have loved and who knew that too.)

And therein lies the significance of an atmospherics of the city, for an atmosphere is that which, like noise and like allegory, can be both perceived and rendered perceptible to others, but without such a revelation giving access to actual or positive knowledge: it disalienates, in that way, and it heightens awareness—but it does not, and cannot, abolish alienation itself. For alienation is a given. And if the readability of allegory is the rhetorical instrument of disalienation, then, dispelling illusion without producing knowledge, it is never entirely free of that other rhetorical *figure de pensée* that is irony—the irony inherent in perceiving that one can be disillusioned without achieving genuine knowledge. Such, then, is the nature of the foggy atmosphere, exemplified perhaps by the one described in "Les sept vieillards," into which modernity—experienced as a becoming conscious of humanity's long fall into the nightmare of history—has plunged us and in which we are condemned to live. An atmosphere, however, that Baudelaire persists in believing can inspire a form of beauty.

The Noisy Fetish

The process that brought Baudelaire to a poetics of allegory and of irony—that is, to an alliance with noise and its principal locus, the riverine streets—began in the fetishizing aesthetics of ideal(izing) beauty that he initially shared with other writers of his generation: such figures as Gautier, Nerval, and even, in his own deeply ironic way, Flaubert. For, being itself the product of urban artifice, the dynamics of fetish is inevitably complex and unstable.

In the case of aesthetic fetishism, such instability arises from the idea of art as redemptive in relation to the ordinary, the banal, the everyday, and the ugly: the familiar reality of disenchanted, that is, modern, urban existence. Such an idea presupposes an artistic engagement with precisely the dreary features of noisy materiality out of which the harmonious ideality of the beautiful is held to emerge. Attention, framing, the work of form can endow an old shoe or a block of wood worked into an interesting shape, be it incongruous or elegant, with the acquired aura that (re)defines it as a fetish object, desirable in certain cases, awesome in others. But it remains true nevertheless that the material object in question is and remains just a piece of well-worn footwear or potential firewood. The fetish is a noisy phenomenon because its structure ensures in this way that it is at odds with itself. To put it in twentieth-century terms, the *negentropy* of (structured) harmony and the *entropy* of (unstructured) materiality are mutually entailed, locked in a kind of embrace, negentropic harmony and entropic noisiness being each crucial to the other's definition. Simultaneously beguilingly attractive (or fearsome) and self-evidently banal, vulgar, and even repellent, the fetish object is an inherently noisy phenomenon in that it combines into an inseparable embrace qualities—such as the beautiful and the ugly, the desirable and the undesirable—that are normally understood to be incompatible (although, as Derrida would add, they are in reality only different, as the fetish itself demonstrates).

Baudelaire is conscious of this paradoxical character of the fetish and, always delighted to *épater le bourgeois*, makes use of it in some "explosive" epigrams, what he calls *pétards* or firecrackers. Aware, for example, that the atmospherics of color, gloss, and light is not limited to the art of painting, he claims that a gaudily painted wooden toy provides the beginning of a child's aesthetic education. Elsewhere he implies strongly that at the theater the chandelier may be a much more compelling object of attention than the goings-on on stage.[13] His point might be formulated more laboriously as follows. If, as I have argued, it is thanks to the factitious character of urban existence as a historical phenomenon—its substitution of streets for rivers—that the artificial supernaturalism of fetish aesthetics comes to define the character of art, superseding the natural supernaturalism of the Romantic sublime, then this would be precisely because, as a man-made environment, the city can offer, as substitutes for the nature that is now absent, only such categories as the material, the useful, and the ordinary. Such categories (exemplified by the street) are already one step away from nature and, by that token, closer—in all their ugliness—than natural objects might be to the *modern* art that seeks to transcend them and to endow them with a saving aura or atmosphere, and is able to do so, moreover, only by means of a further artifice—a purely material intervention—of its own: the work of form. Ergo, utilitarian objects like toys and chandeliers can, on occasion, themselves mimic the effect of a work of art and exert a fascination comparable to that of a painting or a statue at the *Salon,* or indeed a poem, which is the burden of Baudelaire's *pétards.* But conversely, art itself cannot be fully separable from the everyday objects that it seeks to transform.

In short, there is not only a complex juggling of the everyday and the beautiful, the harmonious and the noisy, to be performed, but also a range of possible emphases within that dynamics, more or less noisiness implying less or more harmony. Thus, Baudelaire begins, as we will see, by stressing the magic of form, of *poiesis* and aesthetic shaping as a negentropic force, in the task of redeeming the distressing formlessness of the material world of modernity, a world perceived as the domain of the antisublime, that is, of the ordinary, the ugly, the vulgar, the noisy. At this stage he is close, in particular, to the kind of aesthetic idealism of which Gautier was the most prominent proponent. But under the impact of political events of considerable violence—the uprisings of February and June 1848, and the bloody repression of the latter of the two together with their increasingly distasteful sequel and the installation of a bourgeois-controlled and capitalistic Second Empire—Baudelaire's tune changes. His awareness of the street—and of the power and strange atmospheric beauty, the compelling force, of a world now seen to be governed by the presence, sometimes occult sometimes manifest, of that which you and I might now term entropy but which Baudelaire describes as history—begins to push him in the direction of a supernaturalism still, but a supernaturalism of noise, or of what more judgmentally he calls "le Mal." And he therefore launches in his late poems into the pursuit of a form that would, paradoxically enough, be attuned to the threatening disintegration, the becoming-*formless,* of the world he now sees around him.

Such a form would no longer be at the service of an illusory comfort. Rather it would be the aesthetic equivalent of an ethical "conscience dans le Mal" that, as I have said, has by his final years become the poet's abiding principle. The name of this form, still fetishistic in its supernaturalism but now a fetishism of noise understood as the perceptible face of an occult force of evil and destruction manifested in history, is allegory. In the great poems of "Tableaux parisiens" written around 1859–61, poetic allegory as an agent of disalienation has displaced the illusory harmonian fetishism of an earlier, more optimistic and utopian moment, now dismissed (although it remains, of course, as the very source of the new mood of intense disillusionment, in the way that in *Les Fleurs du Mal* spleen displaces but does not supplant the ideal, which itself supplements but never fully substitutes for spleen).

And that same ideal-spleen relation of interchangeability—of difference without disconnection—governs Baudelaire's partial turn, begun in the middle to late 1850s, to prose poetry and its concomitant figure of irony. Both allegory and irony are tropes of recognition, *figures de pensée* (figures of thought) in the terminology of French rhetoric, as opposed to *figures de mots* (verbal figures). Each, that is, is textually inexplicit, allegory optionally so but irony obligatorily—a matter not of statement ("this is an allegory," "I am working an irony here") but of implication, that is of readability. But in Baudelaire's perspective, irony (and poetic prose) seem to lie at the *spleen* pole of what is in any case more a continuum than a dichotomy, while verse poetry and allegory occupy the *ideal* end, irony being understood as "writing made noisy" while the allegorical function of Baudelaire's late verse makes the noisiness of the world its object of indexical reference much more than its medium. The verse medium itself, in these allegorical poems, remains broadly speaking harmonian, given its continued adherence to conventions of rhythm and rhyme, so that its reference to the cosmic noisiness that governs the historical world occurs within an overall frame of orderly writing in which strategic outbreaks of local disorder subserve an indicative function and provide interpretive clues.[14]

So the reader of allegorical verse recognizes noisiness as the ugly and frightening dimension of a reading experience that presents itself as shrouded in the still beautifying, redemptive, "upward-turning" atmospherics of poetic beauty, an atmospherics still reminiscent, therefore, of the idealizing function of Baudelaire's earlier, largely pre-1848, aesthetics. But in the case of poetic prose, irony—assuming it is perceived—makes reading itself a direct experience of noise, and thus a directly disalienating (or consciousness-raising) encounter with an actual experience of alienation, a foreshadowing of the Brechtian *Verfremdungseffekt.* Atmospherics, here—that of the text and that of the city—is now a purely immanent phenomenon, without obvious transcendent implication, and thus what I would term a *downward-trending* phenomenon, in that it is understood as confined to the level of daily experience. The city's atmosphere arises now merely as a consequence of such a defamiliarizing perception, whereby the *aura* of strangeness that may attach to ordinary things no longer necessarily implies a transcendental *beyond.*

It follows that the famous aphorism of *Fusées* XI—"Deux qualités littéraires fondamentales: surnaturalisme et ironie" (*OC* 1:658; two fundamental literary qualities: supernaturalism and irony)—is itself deeply ironic, given that the two qualities declared to be fundamental to aesthetic writing are so dissimilar as to be inimical, the one implying (for Baudelaire) a transcendental structure of the world, the other its possible or probable absence. It is thus the famous "droit de se contredire" that allows one to alternate between them, as does Baudelaire in moving between verse and prose. Nevertheless, this tension of the ironical and the allegorical modes—one associated with prose, the other with verse—is fundamental to the work of the late Baudelaire and to its significance, making the corpus itself a noisy one, and showing him to be an inheritor not solely of Wordsworthian sublimity (at first reduced to the artificial supernaturalism of fetish aesthetics and later transformed in the allegorical poems into a transcendentalism of the malign) but also of German Romanticism, with its insistence—whether formulated as Hölderlin's "alternation of tones" (*Wechsel der Töne*) or as Friedrich Schlegel's more famous "permanent digressivity" (*permanente Parekbasis*)—on the constant breaking of the frame that is irony.

As for Baudelaire's succession, it necessarily includes the modernist fascination with cities (Joyce, Eliot et al.) as well as the tradition of Paris poetry that runs through the twentieth century, from Apollinaire to Roubaud and Réda. But more appositely, in the context of an atmospherics of noise, there are those who have invested, poetically or otherwise, in the power of disorder, dissolution and waste: Rimbaud's visionary "dérèglement de *tous les sens*" (disruption of *each and every sense*), or Bataille's commitment to a sovereignty, beyond the mastery-subjection dialectic and achievable through expenditure, or *dépense*. Finally, those closest to Baudelaire are doubtless the many modern poets—as well as painters and musicians—who have dedicated their art to a paradoxical engagement with what Baudelaire would have called "l'Ennemi" and identified with the city. I mean the inventors of a poetics of the antipoetic—of negativity, disharmony, distress, destruction. These are more concerned with a certain need to bear witness than with the impossible construction of an aesthetically and philosophically harmonious *oeuvre* supposedly exempt from the ravages of the real—of time and its noisy partner: entropy. For a poetics of noise such as the one we will follow Baudelaire in the process of inventing, is necessarily dedicated to a certain kind of failure, but a failure that is also—in its own way and as a demonstration of what is entailed in the pursuit of veracity—a certain kind of testimonial success. In this respect, Paul Celan is in a tradition of poetic witnessing whose founder was Baudelaire.

However, my present concern is not so much to trace the long and complex becoming-noisy of nineteenth- and twentieth-century aesthetics, via the turn from nature to the city and the fetish aesthetics it engendered. More simply, I want to reflect on the stakes of Baudelaire's particular engagement with noise as the key to an atmospherics of the city. My reflection will take the form of careful readings of a small group of poems, all of which were assigned by Baudelaire to the new "Tableaux parisiens" section that he introduced in the 1860 edition of *Les Fleurs du Mal,* or else formed part of the *Nachlaß* of prose poems that were collected, after his death, in the volume now most frequently referred to as *Le Spleen de Paris.*

It is evident that such a project cannot be a Rankean how-it-really-was history, given the scatter of poems and other documents that remain to us as evidence of a career passionately devoted to art at a time of painfully rapid and indeed traumatic historical and cultural transition: the transformation of a France still largely rural at the time of Baudelaire's birth into a bourgeois, capitalist, industrial, and urban civilization, amid political and social upheavals to match the violence of economic and cultural change. Think of the chapters that follow, then, as constituting an *'istoria* in the ancient sense—an after-the-event "investigation" into "what happened" in an imaginable but otherwise fundamentally irretrievable past. Or as a Benjaminian allegory, a melancholic reflection or *Andenken* pursued among some surviving fragments that bear witness to the disaster that Baudelaire lived as the modernization of France.

TWO

The Magic Windowpane

If, as I have suggested, Baudelaire is at the cusp of a transition in aesthetic history from a literature of the communicable—whose condition is the denegation of noise—to a literature of unlimited readability, grounded in a confrontation with noise as the poetic other, our starting point lies in the fetish aesthetics of early to mid-nineteenth-century France, under the aegis of a theory of "ideal beauty." If the Romantic sublime functioned as what M. H. Abrams baptized "natural supernaturalism"—an aesthetics turned by definition toward the natural environment and implying wonderment or awe as its most appropriate response—fetish beauty, in contrast, is associated with life in the new industrial and commercial cities, such as London or Paris. As a supernaturalism of the urban everyday, it was a new form of (pseudo)transcendence, one dependent for its effect—unlike the sublime—on artifice, that is, on human agency.

In fetish aesthetics, wonderment is still tinged with a sense of the sacred, then. But it also seems less associated with responses of awe, wonderment, or sublime terror than with a purely aesthetic and reflective enjoyment: beauty experienced and appreciated, that is, as a form of the *desirable,* and consequently tinged as much with erotic and even commercial desirability as with a religious or quasi-religious response in the presence of the transcendent. In this way, aesthetic fetishism—which was never so named or perhaps even recognized as such in the period itself—has features that associate it in one way with religious fetishism, already identified in the Enlightenment era, but in others with erotic fetishism, a phenomenon first identified by Rétif de la Bretonne but not formally acknowledged until the era of Alfred Binet and Sigmund Freud. And finally the fetishism of commodities famously identified by Marx in *Das Kapital* (1867) is also entirely relevant.[1]

In writers such as Nerval and Flaubert, then, what we would now call fetishism, never identified as such, is clearly *described* and frequently associated at the same time with a tension between the countryside and the "modern" environment of Paris which had already begun to make rural life seem dated, provincial, and old-fashioned. But in these writers there is also clear discomfort about the relation of an idealizing understanding of beauty to the perceived vulgarity of fetishistic desire and its objects. Desire like that of Emma Bovary, for instance, or of the narrator of "Sylvie," who describes with some precision the dynamics of fetish when he writes: "Aimer une religieuse sous la forme d'une actrice" (To love a nun in the shape of an actress), and adds: "il y a de quoi devenir fou" (is enough to drive one mad).[2] For here, *beauty* understood as the desirable is less a given, and a sublime manifestation of the sacred (for which in

Nerval's story the lost Adrienne is a figure) than it is a phenomenon both strange and artificial—manufactured, as it were, by devices and tricks of art, and thus a matter of *technè* or, in Nerval's telling turn of phrase, of *forme*. For *forme* is a word that applies simultaneously, here, to the practice of *artistic* form (Aurélie's costuming, as a device of the theatrical) and to the shapely *physical* figure of the actress. Nerval's allegory in "Sylvie" is thus clearly legible: urban art, that of Aurélie, has something simultaneously disturbing and vulgar about it, something that distinguishes it, as acting or stagecraft, *both* from the natural simplicity of a country Sylvie (when she was young) and from the sublimity of the sacred, which is associated with the saintly nun Adrienne, now lost to death. Aurélie's material body, heightened as it is by aesthetic artifice, strangely recalls the sacred and offers itself as a substitute for it, even though, as forms of beauty, they are as incompatible as a strutting actress plying her trade and a nun.

What I will want to suggest in what follows, then, is that if Baudelaire's intervention in the history of idealizing fetish aesthetics, understood as a function of artistic form, entails a similar sense of artificiality, and hence of misfit or incongruity, then we can trace what seems to have been, in him, a growing mistrust of an art of the ideal dependent on techniques that could produce only an illusion of compatibility between levels of experience as distant as a sense of the sacred and the material triviality of the urban everyday. Baudelaire's apparently effortless mastery of such an art of proximity is beautifully illustrated by the early poem: "Je n'ai pas oublié . . ." (poem 99), which went unpublished until 1857 and was incorporated into the "Tableaux parisiens" section of the 1861 edition of *Les Fleurs du Mal*, as if it was in some sense a poem of Paris.[3] But in it we can also detect the source of the poet's future discontent with an aesthetic of fetishistic illusionism that is tellingly associated, here, with the transforming, purifying and even sacralizing—but also deceptive—magic of nostalgia.

"Je n'ai pas oublié . . ."

> Je n'ai pas oublié, voisine de la ville,
> Notre blanche maison, petite mais tranquille;
> Sa Pomone de plâtre et sa vieille Vénus
> Dans un bosquet chétif cachant leurs membres nus,
> Et le soleil, le soir, ruisselant et superbe,
> Qui, derrière la vitre où se brisait sa gerbe,
> Semblait, grand œil ouvert dans le ciel curieux,
> Contempler nos dîners longs et silencieux,
> Répandant largement ses beaux reflets de cierge
> Sur la nappe frugale et les rideaux de serge.
>
> (I have not forgotten the house we lived in then,
> it was just outside of town, a little white house
> in a skimpy grove that hid the naked limbs
> of plaster goddesses—the Venus was chipped!
> Nor those seemingly endless evenings when the sun
> whose rays ignited every windowpane
> seemed, like a wide eye in the wondering sky,
> to contemplate our long silent meals,
> kindling more richly than any candlelight
> the cheap curtains and the much-laundered cloth.)

Let us begin, then, with the denegation of time in line 1 of this idealizing poem. To say "Je n'ai pas oublié" is not the same as saying "Je me souviens" (I remember). Time's entropic effect is being specifically *denied* here, in a statement that therefore simultaneously *acknowledges* that effect, by recognizing the fact of forgetting. And the careful balancing of the opening alexandrine's two hemistichs associates the denial of time with the idea of *voisinage,* or vicinity. Spatial proximity functions as an agent of the form of temporal denial, the denial of distance in time, that is called nostalgia, a word the poem does not need to use because it is implicit in the overemphatic antiphrasis of the opening words. (Antiphrasis often works in French as an intensifier.) The proximity to the city of the remembered "blanche maison" (situated, as we know from the biographical evidence, in what was then the village of Neuilly), cancels time's distance, while the rhyme that associates *ville* and *tranquille* simultaneously contrasts the tranquil house with the implied bustle and busyness of life in town, which is thus indirectly indicated as the site of the speaker's nostalgic reminiscing.

But proximity is also the crucial device of fetishizing, as Freud pointed out. For an inaccessible object of desire, the fetishizing subject substitutes, by metonymy, an accessible but also proximate alternative—a shoe, a garter, or a stocking displaces the unattainable sexual organ, for instance—so that the substitute object acquires, as its aura or atmosphere, the desirable properties of the true object of desire that is beyond reach. Indeed there is, as it were, an exchange of properties, as the desirable acquires the property of attainability while the attainable, which might otherwise be despised as ordinary, familiar, and without interest, becomes desirable in its turn. In this way, the Neuilly of many summers ago becomes close, while noisy Paris benefits from the remembered innocence and calm of the "blanche maison" (notice the hint of purity in the preposed adjective *blanche*). But if this is the mechanism of fetish, the fact that it *is* a mechanism or device (a trope) simultaneously admits the possibility of partial or complete malfunctioning, that is, of noise—a form of static or interference that can be ignored, but which *needs* to be ignored because it threatens the system of illusion from within.

And in the same way, this poem's overall function is to bring about, by means of a poetic operation that mimes the enhancing effect of nostalgic memory, a kind of fetishizing redemption, whereby the *banality* and shabby poverty of what, in Baudelaire's youth, was not quite yet the *banlieue* (the two words are etymologically related) become suffused in a transformative light, while poetic noise is similarly dispelled by harmonious sound. In this way, what the poem describes as nostalgic enhancement is also what it performs, on its own behalf, through the work of its poetic form; and what is "chétif" (line 3) or "frugale" (line 10) is rendered generous and beautiful (line 9: "beaux reflets de cierge"), this effect being ascribed to the largesse of the setting sun—but also to the refraction of a "vitre" (line 6). It is as if a supernatural source of light, figured by a natural phenomenon, joins forces with an artificial verbal intervention that doubles for and enacts the work of poetic form, and in so doing produces an effect of *semblance* (cf. "semblait," line 7), the sun adapting its transcendence to a more human scale as it comes to "seem" a contemplative eye (line 5), while the human dwelling is bathed in the transformative light of the beyond. The "nappe frugale" and the "rideaux de serge" are made over by the "nappe de lumière"—the phrase is inescapable—resulting from the work of the sun and the windowpane, and the resulting glow produces an aura of the sacred. (It is necessary to remember that nineteenth-century glass was quite faulty and contained bubbles of air, so that the glow would be that of warm summer evening sunshine dappled by the glass like the "reflets de cierge" of line 9, suggestive of religious ceremony). Meanwhile the poem's own frugal rhyme of lines 3–4 ("Vénus" / "nus" is technically a "rime pauvre," impoverished rhyme, or even a "rime suffisante," sufficient rhyme) is similarly redeemed by the harmonian wealth, the generosity of the hemistich-long "rhyming" of "ses beaux reflets de cierge" with "et les rideaux de serge" (not just "cierge" / "serge," but also "de cierge" / "de serge"; "beaux" and "rideaux"; "ses" and "les" together with a 4/2 distribution of the rhythmic accent pattern in each of the paired hemistichs). And the instrumental "vitre" displays its own relation to the poem (understood) as performing the magic of *poiesis,* in that it is recognizably a phonetic amalgam of consonants from line 3 ("plâtre," "vieille Vénus") and the rhyme vowel "i" of lines 1–2 ("ville" / "tranquille"). As a form of artifice, it derives from the *urban* environment, and like the statues of the garden, it is a product of *art.*

And the *vitre,* the statues, and the sun will all reappear in Baudelaire's later poetry, albeit in a transformed guise. The benign and generous divinity will acquire a more sinister and threatening visage, or rather will yield to a re-envisioning of the sacred in terms, now of *le Mal.* And the garden statues will make a reappearance—once Baudelaire has revised the opinion of statuary he expresses in the *Salon de 1846*—as something like emissaries of this new, disastrous, divinity: awe-inspiring allegorical figures with power to shock, dismay, and dispel comfortable illusions. Similarly, where the sun is a welcome supper guest in the Neuilly poem, the "Pomone de plâtre" and the "vieille Vénus"—as themselves domesticated representations of pre-Christian divinities demurely concealing their "membres nus"—will come to be viewable, in retrospect, as having foreshadowed the statue of the Commendatore in Mozart and da Ponte's *Don Giovanni,* a key figure in Baudelaire's imaginary, who demonstrates the uncanny power of *walking* in order to make a visit of retribution at a more festive supper than the domestic meal in "Je n'ai pas oublié . . . ." And, in the same retrospective view, the dappling of the sun's evening glow by the windowpane seems to look forward to the *spectrality* of the apparitions that emerge out of the city's noisy atmosphere in some of Baudelaire's great poems of 1859–61, most evidently the "spectre en plein jour" (daylight specter) of "Les sept vieillards" (see line 2).

My claim in later chapters will be, then, that the transformed figures of the statuesque that emerge over time in Baudelaire's poetic imagination—the *passante* (passerby), the swan/Andromache, the *vieillards* (old men)—are not solely manifestations of the sinister sacrality that was to supersede in his writing the benign divinity of the sun, but also manifestations whose refracting medium is no longer the magic windowpane but the city noise that constitutes the atmosphere of Paris and will become the new medium of a sacred of *le Mal*. That is why, for my argument, the most significant moment in all Baudelaire is in the prose poem, "Le mauvais vitrier" ("The Bad Glazier"), when the poet narrator throws his window wide open to the noise of the city, in a gesture that encapsulates Baudelaire's own (never complete) renunciation of the magical refracting windowpane of idealizing aesthetics in favor of an atmospherics of noise—one that, by this time, will have shed its supernatural reference completely.[4] Such a gesture represents the inevitable return, within a fetishizing aesthetics, of the inescapable but repressed component of the ordinary and the unbeautiful that makes the fetish such a noisy phenomenon, jostling the mundane and the sublime into uncomfortable proximity.

In such a light, the "vicinity" of urban Paris to the "blanche maison" of "Je n'ai pas oublié . . ." is of a piece with the copresence in the poem (indeed the carefully symmetrical positioning) of the moment of noisy rhyme that is the "Vénus" / "nus" stumble and of the plethoric hemistichs that seek to repair or redeem it at the poem's end. For just as the stumble at lines 4–5 constitutes noise only because it is positionally presented as a rhyme—one that passes muster by benefiting from a technicality—the final magnificent hemistichs do not technically rhyme at all (except for the final words). If the words that stumble were not placed at the line-ends, they would count as part of the harmonious word music at which this poem excels; and inversely the (pseudo)rhyming at lines 9–10 might be more accurately described as word music rather than what I called "hemistich rhyming." For (like word music) it too incorporates plenty of parasitic noise: "reflets" and "rideaux" do not rhyme, although the words clearly resemble each other in certain ways, and the repetitious "de" at syllable 11 of each alexandrine, like the mismatched syllabic pair "ses beaux" / "et les" at the "attaque" of each hemistich (i.e., at syllables 7–8) produces a kind of stutter that is mitigated only by the sweeping rhythmic patterning and the fact that such utilitarian words as *et, ses,* and *de* always tend to pass unnoticed in any overall effect of splendor, just as they do in word music. They are "just" background static.

If we recognize this presence of noise in the poem as a signal, however, we can see that the poem is intimating here its recognition of the inseparability of harmony and noise, order and disorder, the beautiful and the ugly in poetry whose relation to the transcendence of a manifestly unattainable sacred—here the munificence of the sun's natural light, "ruisselant et superbe"—must inevitably be a matter of artifice. That is, the relation must be mediated, for example, by the refractive magic of an intervening "vitre" that can produce only "*reflets* de cierge," and whose phonetic relation to the garden statuary we noticed a moment ago. The shabby statues and the magic windowpane are forms of art, then; and indeed of modern art: the art of a world itself become modern and whose nostalgia for a sense of the sacred no longer available betrays that unfamiliar world's lost connection to a tradition now become irrelevant. A disenchanted art of artificial re-enchantment, then, and one plagued by "noise within the system."

But we can glimpse something of Baudelaire's sense of a path forward—more by way of further exploration of a recalcitrant problem, I suggest, than as a matter of real progress—in two post-1848 poems that had appeared in the 1857 *Fleurs du Mal* but were then artfully regrouped and repositioned in 1861, following the trial that Baudelaire had found so painful, so as to signify in relation one to the other. Placed now at the liminal position of the new "Tableaux parisiens" section, they read in sequence as enacting a renunciation of idealizing art—the art figured by the windowpane—and define a new relation to the sun, one that is programmatic for this whole group of poems concerning Paris.

"Paysage" and "Le Soleil"

> Sans prendre garde à l'ouragan
> Qui fouettait mes vitres fermées,
> Moi, j'ai fait *Emaux et Camées.*
>
> (Without noticing the hurricane
> that lashed my closed windowpane,
> I wrote *Enamels and Cameos.*)
>
> Théophile Gautier, "Préface," *Emaux et Camées*

Paysage

Je veux, pour composer chastement mes églogues,
Coucher auprès du ciel, comme les astrologues,
Et, voisin des clochers, écouter en rêvant
Leurs hymnes solennels, emportés par le vent.
Les deux mains au menton, du haut de ma mansarde,
Je verrai l'atelier, qui chante et qui bavarde;
Les tuyaux, les clochers, ces mâts de la cité,
Et les grands ciels qui font rêver d'éternité.
Il est doux, à travers les brumes, de voir naître
L'étoile dans l'azur, la lampe à la fenêtre,

Les fleuves de charbon monter au firmament
Et la lune verser son pâle enchantement.
Je verrai les printemps, les étés, les automnes;
Et quand viendra l'hiver aux neiges monotones,
Je fermerai partout portières et volets
Pour bâtir dans la nuit mes féeriques palais.
Alors, je rêverai des horizons bleuâtres,
Des jardins, des jets d'eau pleurant dans les albâtres,
Des baisers, des oiseaux chantant soir et matin,
Et tout ce que l'Idylle a de plus enfantin.
L'Émeute, tempêtant vainement à ma vitre,
Ne fera pas lever mon front de mon pupitre;
Car je serai plongé dans cette volupté
D'évoquer le Printemps avec ma volonté,
De tirer un soleil de mon cœur, et de faire
De mes pensers brûlants une tiède atmosphère.

Parisian Landscape

To make my eclogues proper, I must sleep
hard by heaven—like the astrologers—
and being the belfries' neighbor, hear in my dreams
their solemn anthems fading on the wind.
My garret view, perused attentively,
reveals the workshops and their singing slaves,
the city's masts—steeples and chimneypots—
and above that fleet, a blue eternity.

How sweet to see the first star in the sky,
the first lamp at the window through the mist,
the coalsmoke streaming upward, and the moon
shedding a pale enchantment on it all!
From there I'll watch the easy seasons pass
and when the tedious winter snows me in,
I'll close my shutters, draw the curtains snug,
and build my Spanish castles in the dark,

dreaming of alluring distances,
of sobbing fountains and of birds that sing
endless obbligatos to my trysts—
of everything in Idylls that's inane!
A revolution down in the street will not
distract me from my desk, for I shall be
committed to that almost carnal joy
of fastening the springtime to my will,
drawing the sun from my heart, and by my zeal
persuading Paris to become a South.

Le Soleil

Le long du vieux faubourg, où pendent aux masures
Les persiennes, abri des secrètes luxures,
Quand le soleil cruel frappe à traits redoublés
Sur la ville et les champs, sur les toits et les blés,
Je vais m'exercer seul à ma fantasque escrime,
Flairant dans tous les coins les hasards de la rime,
Trébuchant sur les mots comme sure les pavés,
Heurtant parfois des vers depuis longtemps rêvés.

Ce père nourricier, ennemi des chloroses,
Éveille dans les champs les vers comme les roses;
Il fait s'évaporer les soucis vers le ciel,
Et remplit les cerveaux et les ruches de miel.
C'est lui qui rajeunit les porteurs de béquilles
Et les rend gais et doux comme des jeunes filles,
Et commande aux moissons de croître et de mûrir
Dans le cœur immortel qui toujours veut fleurir!

Quand, ainsi qu'un poète, il descend dans les villes,
Il ennoblit le sort des choses les plus viles,
Et s'introduit en roi, sans bruit et sans valets,
Dans tous les hôpitaux et dans tous les palais.

The Sun

Late in this cruel season when the sun
scourges alike the city and the fields,
parching the stubble and sinking into slums
where shuttered hovels hide vile appetites,
I venture out alone to drill myself
in what must seem an eerie fencing-match,
dueling in dark corners for a rhyme
and stumbling over words like cobblestones
where now and then realities collide
with lines I dreamed of writing long ago.

What greensickness could stand up to the sun,
that towering foster father who dissolves
anxieties into air like morning mist,
ripening here a verse and there a rose
with honey on the tongue as in the hive?
Who but the sun persuades the lame to dance
as if their canes were maypoles, governing
the resurrection of the harrowed fields,
and for the secret harvest of the heart
commands immortal wheat to grow again!

When, with a poet's will, the sun descends
into the cities like a king incognito,
impartially visiting palace and hospital,
the fate of all things vile is glorified.

The *descente dans la rue* enacted by means of these two poems entails a leave-taking, then, from the idealizing poetry of the *vitre*. This word, featured in "Je n'ai pas oublié . . . ," had figured prominently in 1851, in the liminal "Préface" to *Emaux et Camées* by Théophile Gautier. But in Gautier it functions as a signifier of aesthetic autonomy from the storms ("l'ouragan") of history; and Baudelaire's line, "L'Emeute, tempêtant vainement à ma vitre," positioned toward the end of "Paysage," clearly refers to Gautier's poem, and endorses its purport, leaving the immediate proximity of "Le Soleil" to imply irony, contestation, or debate of any kind between the two poets.[5] For the debate, in fact, seems rather to concern more directly the word *atmosphère,* which, figuring as the last word of "Paysage," looks forward from there to "Le Soleil"—again implicitly—by virtue of the subjectivist implications of the couplet that encapsulates the tenor of the whole poem it concludes. Baudelaire, I think, does not wish to contest Gautier's aesthetics *directly*. He prefers, for fairly obvious reasons (such as his friendship and prominently expressed admiration for the celebrated and successful "Théo"), to do so by working a kind of irony by juxtaposition. As a consequence, the crucial problem that is never made explicit in all this careful distancing on Baudelaire's part is that of the relation of poetry to history. But the reference to the storm in both Gautier's poem and Baudelaire's alludes unmistakably to the events of 1848 and their sequel.[6]

Having referenced Gautier in this way by invoking his protective *vitre,* "Paysage" goes on, then, to define idealizing poetry—poetry written under the protection of the windowpane—in terms of a certain voluptuousness, "cette volupté"

> De tirer un soleil de mon coeur, et de faire
> De mes pensers brûlants une tiède atmosphère.

It will be around this question of the relation of poetry and the poet to the sun that the debate between "Paysage" and "Le Soleil" will be explicitly staged. In "Paysage," the sun is recruited, indeed co-opted, somewhat as it was in "Je n'ai pas oublié . . . "; but now it is as if it were at best the poet's coadjutor, and at worst (since it is winter) his absentee assistant, one whose temporary defection can be readily compensated for by the production of the subjective warmth that creates, it seems, an entirely artificial, fabricated atmosphere. And it is this stuffy, subjective, and self-enclosed atmosphere—"Je fermerai partout portières et volets"—that by implication "Le soleil" rejects. It does so first by staging the springtime return of "le soleil cruel" after its eclipse by the season of fogs and of moonlight, and second by reposing the question of poetic making (the aesthetic production of "atmosphere") in the objectivist terms of the (sunlit) city street. What place can there be for a *vitre*—whether magic in its function or protective—when the poet descends into the street and, in doing so, finds he must face up to an encounter with history, the product of time and contingency, instead of turning from it and taking refuge in an idealizing poetry that denies these forces?

"Paysage"

In "Paysage," then, the poet in his garret with his eye to the windowpane is capable of replacing the sun (which itself was a "grand oeil ouvert dans le ciel curieux" in "Je n'ai pas oublié . . ."); and thus of embracing a contemplative stance and a panoramic perspective. Such a stance is able—notably in winter, and at night—to bring the "cité" (line 7) into idealizing proximity with "les grands ciels qui font rêver d'éternité" (line 8). Furthermore, city poetry of this kind is compatible—precisely because it is idealizing—with pastoral genres and modes ("mes églogues," line 1), and this by virtue of an ability that, in "Le Soleil," will be attributed to the sun alone: that of shining equally, with its "traits redoublés," on city and country alike ("la ville et les champs," line 4), and consequently *ennobling*—note the monarchical metaphor—"les choses les plus viles" (line 18). And finally, this spatial proximity of city and country underlies an even more fundamental function of idealizing, subjective, and long-distance vision, that of denying the relevance of time: for the poet looking out over the city all year long, winter simply becomes the season when poetic imagination ("Je rêverai," line 7) supplants the absent sun, so that the poet's idyllic and idealizing vision of the city—in which plumes of industrial smoke become "fleuves de charbon," for example—may continue uninterrupted:

> Je verrai les printemps, les étés, les automnes,
> Et quand viendra l'hiver
> ....
> Je fermerai partout portières et volets
> Pour bâtir dans la nuit mes féeriques palais

This gift for creating a "tiède atmosphere" out of his own subjectivity (his "pensers brûlants," line 26) is something the poet has apparently learned from this experience of night as the absence of sunshine, and more particularly from autumn mists, starlight, and the nocturnal moon (which is, of course, like an alternative sun in its power to "verser son pâle enchantement," line 12). That is why there is a clear semantic correspondence between the opening lines of the poem's second section ("Il est doux, à travers les *brumes,* de *voir naître / L'étoile dans l'azur*") and its closing lines:

> De *tirer un soleil de mon coeur,* et de faire
> De mes pensers *brû*lants une tiède atmosphère.

But this final shift into subjective mode also implies, most tellingly of all, a new function for *la vitre,* which now ceases to be an instrument of poeticizing vision ("voir naître," line 9; "Je verrai," line 13) as in a sense it had already been in "Je n'ai pas oublié . . . ," to become purely protective, shielding the poet at his "pupitre" (line 22) from the tempests of history. And it is *this* subjectivizing *vitre,* then, with its unmistakable echo of Gautier, that will be ironized by the juxtaposition of "Paysage" with "Le Soleil," as I have already suggested.

"Le Soleil"

Abandoning the *vitre,* then, together with the contemplative posture and the denial of time to which "Je n'ai pas oublié . . ." had already subscribed (while assigning to the windowpane a refractive role, however, that implied a more humble stance on the part of the poet toward the majestic sun), "Le Soleil" retains the kingly power and generosity ascribed to the sun in that earlier poem, albeit implicitly diminished in "Paysage" by the poem's promotion of the poet's autonomy. "Le Soleil" does so, however, to present the relation of the poet to the sun quite differently from both of these previous poems, although contrasting most markedly with "Paysage." For now the poet measures his own poetic powers against those of the sun quite explicitly, and in a relation of quasi-rivalry. He does this by comparing them to those of the sun in relation to the crucial poetic practice of rhyme, which now becomes explicitly thematic (whereas in "Je n'ai pas oublié . . ." it had appeared only as a nonthematized practice, and as something like the "reflets de cierge" of that poem—like them, I mean, in the sense that it appeared there as a merely *imitative* or *derived* way of conveying the idealizing power of sunlight, itself only softened and refracted by virtue of its objective correlative: the "vitre").

No longer "voisin des clochers" but descending instead into the street, the poet pursues his atmospherics of the city under the dreary conditions defined by the "vieux faubourg," with its hanging shutters and the vulgarity of its "secrètes luxures." There is no longer any prospect of his taking the panoramic, distancing view. That privilege, and its power of reconciling nature and culture, the countryside and the modern urban environment, now belong exclusively to the sun, which exercises its magisterial powers of idealizing rhyming in stark contrast with the poet's restriction to the shabby realities of his own, working-class-cum-Bohemian, neighborhood. These include the realities of spatial (cf., "le long du vieux faubourg") and correlatively of temporal extension, within whose constraints he must find a way to work that perfect coincidence of the different—of palaces and poorhouses, kings and valets—that is rhyme.

Understood in this way—and in the absence of the magical windowpane—as a newly explicit figure for fetish aesthetics, rhyme thus becomes the terrain on which the gulf between the powers of the sun and the efforts of the poet to match them become evident. For the sun requires no mediator to do its work of rhyming: it "s'introduit en roi, *sans bruit et sans valets,* / Dans tous les hôpitaux et dans tous les palais." The poet, on the other hand, cannot rhyme except by means of the linguistic mediation that defines verse: his humble work in the street consists of pursuing those elusive "vers depuis longtemps rêvés" that might permit him, "parfois," to imitate, in his own way, the regal work of illumination and ennoblement that sunshine so perfectly and effortlessly achieves. Where the sun works noiselessly, then, and unaided by "servants," the poet must contend with the noise that is the inevitable consequence of the phenomenon of mediation, be it in time or in space. The racket of the noisy city street along which the poet pursues his erratic, stumbling path is correlative to the digressivity required of poetry in its search for perfect rhymes in the world of extension, a world in which immediacy is the exclusive privilege of the sun. That is, the poet must face the stumbling block of randomness and chance, "le hasard." His progress along the street becomes a "fantasque escrime" (line 5), an odd, unpredictable fencing-around that contrasts with the surety of the sun's "traits redoublés" (line 3), the double-striking efficiency of solar swordmanship. And if these fencing metaphors still imply a certain nobility that the poet shares with the sun, that is perhaps thanks only to those miraculous "vers depuis longtemps rêvés" (line 8) that he sometimes encounters. These rare successes notwithstanding, it is the contrast between the "cruel" accuracy and efficiency of solar striking and the uncertainty and randomness, the sheer clumsiness to which the poet is reduced in his dependency on the contingencies of chance, that most surely constitutes the point of the poem. We are truly far from the enchanting world of "Paysage" and its "tiède atmosphère," so readily generated out of "pensers brûlants."

Poetry and Noise

Poetry, then, has become a strange and erratic fencing match. It is no longer fought with the weapon of light, the sun's now exclusive rapier, nor yet with the comfortably subjective illusions of "pensers brûlants," both of these now discarded options being associated with the no longer relevant windowpane. It can only be fought on the plane of rhyme, both with and against words and the things they refer to: recalcitrant words like *pavé* (which, however, just happens to rhyme with the uplifting *rêvé*) as well as noble words like *palais* (which rhymes uncomfortably with *valets*). Or to put it a little more specifically, it is actually verse that constitutes the poet's weaponry, since it is only the *extension* of the line of verse that makes available the resources of both rhyme and rhythm.

For the poet's battling with the contingent has, as it were, a double goal: to acknowledge the noisy, material, sorry reality of the urban, whose microcosm is the (also extended) street in all its barely concealed depravity and all-too-evident haphazard disorder; yet still to produce, out of those unpromising materials, the effect of beauty, through the rhymes and rhythms of verse. Such beauty is understood, fetish fashion, as capable of "ennobling" the vile, in the manner of the sun, by conferring on it an aura that refers to an otherwise inaccessible sphere of transcendent and awe-inspiring, sunlike majesty. So whereas the structure of fetish remains pertinent to Baudelaire's poetic imagination, its structural noise has greatly increased with this new acknowledgement of the sheer inescapable presence of fetish's shabby and vulgar material component. Which means in turn that the fetish has itself become a much noisier phenomenon, less smooth and magical in its working, and newly complicated by awareness of the problematics of mediation. For the necessity of mediation arises in a world of temporal and spatial distance, along with the fact of difference that is its consequence. How, then, to create the desired harmony out of the babble of irreconcilable differences that are, of course, both the consequence and the cause, or motor, of human history?

It is rhyme that presents itself precisely as the outcome of this necessary negotiation of harmony and difference, one that is itself mediated by the intervening metrical line. For, at the cost of introducing distance into the apparent immediacy of the rhyming words, lines of verse—which also rhyme rhythmically, as it were, among themselves—supply the semantic modulation that naturalizes the phonetic and semantic difference of words like *pavé* and *rêvé* or *valets* and *palais*, and thus produces the effect of harmony. They represent the work of form that is crucial to an aesthetics of fetish as a mode of "artificial supernaturalism." The hitch, however, is that *this* magic doesn't always work. As we saw at the mid-point of "Je n'ai pas oublié . . . ," and as a quick check of the rhymes of "Le Soleil" will confirm, rhymes can be ugly, and many are simply banal. Rhyme is subject to *hasard,* rhyming is chancy; and one can only hope to stumble sometimes over a salvific "vers depuis longtemps rêvé," rather than just a paving stone.

But as the existence of such only rare "vers rêvés" testifies, verse is itself as capable of imperfection as rhyme itself; and not coincidentally lines 1 and 2 of "Le Soleil" display how readily verse, like the poet of lines 3–4, can stumble. There is the awkward enjambment of an inverted phrase, perhaps intended to suggest that the shutters are hanging askew; and a line so metrically noisy as to almost defy scansion. In "Le long du vieux faubourg, où pendent aux masures / Les persiennes, abri des secrètes luxures," the second line qualifies as an alexandrine only if "persiennes" counts as three syllables. But if the word is pronounced "per-si-ennes" this result is achieved at the cost of a classically frowned upon (but not strictly forbidden) unpronounced silent e immediately preceding the caesura. And alternatively, if "persiennes" becomes "per-sien-nes," pronouncing the final e, it becomes necessary (in order to avoid an ugly hiatus) to make the liaison with "abri," across the intervening comma, with the result that the line now finds itself both equipped with an extra syllable and bereft of its caesura. There are only bad options. Meanwhile the rhyme "masures" / "luxures," far from working a magical redemption of the "masures," simply confirms the irreparable indignity of the neighborhood (hovels shelter licentiousness, which has its natural home in tumbledown living quarters).

True, the four concluding lines of the strophe countermand, and perhaps correct, these opening disasters with metrically correct rhythms and two sets of uplifting rhymes:

> Je vais m'exercer seul à ma fantasque escrime,
> Flairant dans tous les coins les hasards de la rime,
> Trébuchant sur les mots comme sur les pavés,
> Heurtant parfois des vers depuis longtemps rêvés.

Here, "rime" seems to absolve "escrime" from its suggestion of randomness, as "pavés" is transformed by "rêvés," while the metrical regularity is such (6/6; 6/6) that sets of internal paradigmatic equivalences, simultaneously positional and semantic, impose themselves on the attention and form "rhythmic rhymes." In the initial position, "Je vais," and especially "Flairant," "Trébuchant" and "Heurtant," but also (in lines 5–6) "fantasque" and "hasards" in (roughly) equivalent places, and (in lines 7–8) "mots" and "vers" at the caesura—as well, perhaps, as "coins" (line 6)—all form parallels that suggest nonphonetic rhyme in this way. But if these lines exemplify Classical ideals of firmly balanced prosody, they also present poetic work, thematically, as a matter of fencing around, sniffing out, stumbling and bumping into things in ungainly fashion; and it would clearly be an error to assume that this kind of dissonance between the thematic and the prosodic is not intended to signify, as an element of the poem's readability.

For the lines in question clearly lack the regal quality of, say, the final lines of "Je n'ai pas oublié . . ." and, striking one as almost caricatural in relation to their stiff classical model, they hardly qualify as exemplars of "vers depuis longtemps rêvés." This is especially the case if one is mindful of Baudelaire's own professed dream of poetic beauty as a complex, graceful, and subtly moving system, like a ship at sea under full sail.[7] These inadequately beautiful lines are in a relation of structural equivalence with the corresponding quatrain that ends the poem, where it is the sun now that is celebrated and described as descending into the city "ainsi qu'un poète," in order to "ennoblir le sort des choses les plus viles" (in lines 4–6), but *also* as penetrating "en roi" into the city's poorhouses and palaces, which are thus, like the "valets" and "palais" at the rhyme of the final lines, rendered as poetically equivalent by virtue of the sun's suprapoetic power, its "traits redoublés." It is this double identity of the sun—like a poet *and* like a king—that in this poem the human poet has renounced by leaving his garret and stepping out into the street. Along with the sun's related power of reconciling the country and the city by means of its "traits redoublés," he has largely lost even the ability to "ennoble" the urban environment to which he is now confined, obliged as he is to battle with "les hasards de la rime." If, at a time now in the past, ordinary poets could once hope, like the sun, to render the countryside beautiful (or at least to render the beauty of the countryside), the modern poet's action is now reduced to the city, whose poetic treatment, unlike nature, requires precisely those regal privileges that—in contradistinction to the sun—he lacks. He must work, henceforth, with his own, purely human means.

Which is doubtless the point that is driven home by the central strophe. These lines mediate between the strophe devoted to the poet and the strophe devoted to the sun, and they do so—I suggest—by praising the sun's transcendent powers in the mediocre verse of the poet condemned to the city. This new dissonance of the thematic and the formal, recalling (while reversing the terms) that of lines 3–6 by means of the strophe's cheap pastiche of the run-of-mill verse—mediocre versification, unremarkable rhymes, embarrassingly bad puns—thus exemplifies the distance now separating the urban poet's work and that of the sun, the awareness of a virtually unbridgeable distance, itself productive of noise, that arises in a world extended in time and in space, as figured by the city street. Here such dissonance, it seems, is the rule: and successful mediation of the poet-sun gap a hazardous undertaking only rarely crowned with success.[8] The little series of puns is instructive in this respect. They exemplify the kind of simultaneity of double reference (country-city, nature-culture) that is otherwise the sun's prerogative: "vers" refers to earthworms *and* to poetic verse (line 10); "soucis" to cares *and* to marigolds (line 11), while "miel"—although this is not strictly a pun, I think—relates gustatory sweetness and mental balm (line 12). But they are also so facile ("vers"), so contrived ("soucis"), or so banal ("miel") that what they emphasize in the end is the ungainliness of the poet's own *démarche,* corresponding in this way to his lurching progress along the street. Thus they reinforce the general sense of noise and mediocrity that this section conveys.

These mediating lines tell us that noise is the inescapable accompaniment to city life that the poet of the modern must face in his effort to make beauty from the mundane. The question for Baudelaire, in future poems, will be, then, no longer how to produce harmonious verses that deny the presence and power of noise and seek to cancel it out, but rather how to incorporate this defining noisiness of urban life into an aesthetics that might somehow be capable of doing justice to noise's pervasive and inescapable, if mostly ignored, presence. How to envisage a noisy form of beauty, or the beauty of noise? How to produce a certain supernaturalism out of a world no longer benignly governed so much as it is subject to forces of disorder, entropy, and chaos; and this by virtue of its involvement in time, extension, the problematics of mediation, as well—something we have yet to see—as the destructive force that is history?

The outcome of this new quest will be the great poems written in the years 1859–61 that are at the core of the "Tableaux parisiens." In them, we will encounter a new vision of the cosmic structure of the world: one that amends the harmonious worldview so characteristic of the utopian 1840s that Baudelaire came eventually to despise, and substitutes the anguished apprehension of a noisy cosmic environment, one obscurely governed by the sinister supernatural forces of *le mal* and productive of the uncomfortable form of awareness that is disalienation.

This new cosmic vision will retain the fetish structure of a sphere of ordinariness and daily life and an other, inaccessible sphere of the supernatural or the sacred, between which a foggy and uncanny sphere of strangeness, a noisy atmosphere, is on occasion perceptible—an atmosphere to which the poet-become-flâneur is both sensitive and uniquely attentive. But this fetish structure will no longer be subject to a poetics of metaphor, but rather a matter of allegory and chiasmus. Such figures, we can note immediately, are homologous with rhyme (and more closely so than is metaphor) in that they too incorporate the sense of noisiness that arises from the mediation of difference. They are aware of the distance that metaphor seeks to deny. Exit the sun, then, from Baudelaire's world, be it the benign and generous sun of "Je n'ai pas oublié . . ." or the cruel divinity in its regal might—the sun of metaphor—that exercises so accurately its "traits redoublés." And enter the statue, the "spectre en plein jour," the figures of the swan and the *passante,* obscure envoys emerging out of the urban atmosphere as striking objects of encounter, stumbled upon in the street, and as messengers of a distantly glimpsed stratum of transcendence, so remote henceforth as to appear, on occasion, void. But a transcendence that is now understood as sinister and threatening, indeed as punitive, in that its power is revealed most inescapably in the noise and devastation, the rubble of human history: the shambles, for example, that large sections of the old city of Paris were to become in the course of the rapid and radical "modernization" that was undertaken, under the Second Empire, by Baron Haussmann.[9]

PART II

Allegory, History, and the Weather of Time

THREE

Fetishism Becomes Allegory

Artificial supernaturalism, as an aesthetics of the ideal, entails, as we've seen, a denial of time. For that reason, it tends to cultivate a fetishism of near-simultaneity—of proximity in "Je n'ai pas oublié . . ." and of the sun's "traits redoublés" in "Le Soleil"—the effect of which is to efface distance and difference, including spatial differences (country/city; city/suburban village) but also the metaphysical difference separating the ordinary and the everyday from the remote ideal.

Such an effect of *rapprochement* depends, in turn, on poetic practices of indifferentiation for which the model is rhyme, practices whose effect is to produce an aura or atmosphere of the beautiful that lends uncanny dignity and desirability to otherwise unworthy things. Such practices might be thought of as akin to metaphor, the trope that brings together differences without apparent mediation and implies their kinship. However, we have also seen in Baudelaire, along with an increasing awareness of rhyme's hazardousness, a growing awareness of that which is simultaneously denied and acknowledged in poetic indifferentiation, that is, the difference, both temporal and spatial, and consequently the distance, that verse exists to mediate. Noise, then, names the *disharmony* that accompanies—as entropy accompanies all forms of negentropy—every attempt within the sphere of time and the contingent to construct perfectly harmonious functioning systems. And that is why it becomes necessary now to turn to Baudelaire's effort in the latter years of his life to invent an atmospherics not of harmony but of noise, an effort entailing a rediscovery and a reevaluation of time and its various entailments: distance, difference, extension.

A Poetics of Time

> Le quotidien a ce trait essentiel: il ne se laisse pas saisir.
>
> (There is this that is essential about daily life: there is no grasping it.)
>
> Maurice Blanchot, *L'Entretien infini*[1]

Following the disillusioning political events of 1848–51, one begins indeed to see signs in Baudelaire, around the mid-1850s, of an emerging new aesthetic project, one in which the attempted denial of time that governed the now visibly utopian aesthetics of the fetish—giving it the character of an attempted reenchantment of a fatally disenchanted world—is displaced by a new dynamics, one not quite of disillusionment but rather of disalienation. Disillusionment would suggest the abandonment of atmospherics and the supernaturalism it implies in favor of some presumably clear-eyed vision of "how things really are." Disalienation, however, rather than implying an escape from ignorance, arises as an awareness of the power of alienation, and as the consequent consciousness of a human *inability to know*. To be disalienated is not necessarily to know the truth but only to have become aware that we cannot know it, and that we are deceived if we think we do. So the fetishistic aura of aesthetic harmony, suggesting a benign transcendence, becomes the veil that conceals the transcendent from us, a veil that Baudelairean disalienation now identifies with the noisy city atmosphere that most people ignore, suggestive as it is both of a power lying beyond that veil and of our inability to know that power, except in its manifestations. And what changes, then, in the new aesthetic dispensation that occupies Baudelaire's later years, is only the character of those manifestations—no longer benign and harmonious, but noisy, threatening, and destructive—and his consequent reassessment of the concealed force whose action they are understood to represent.

No longer a benign and generous sun, that covert force now becomes the Enemy of humanity, dubbed the Devil or Evil ("le Mal"), and variously represented as the abyss, the "gouffre" or "le sabbat des siècles" (the witches' Sabbath of the centuries). As in the Roman *sacer*, Baudelaire's sacred too proves to have both a dexter and a sinister side: and it is the sinister form of transcendent power that now becomes identified with what, in less religious terms, the third law of thermodynamics calls entropy. The malign transcendent force is now understood, in other words, as the disharmony or noise inherent in every systematic construction, and growing as the system gradually wears away and in time falls into disorder, to be replaced by another system no less subject to disorder and decline. An old rhyme speaks of "time the anthropophagous" which "swallows up each human work."[2] Apparently assuming still the supposedly eternal laws of Nature, it is *this* view of time—as the covertly destructive force that makes a mockery of human progress—

that Baudelaire now associates with the city, and hence with modernity, and promotes to the status of supernatural power.

After the early poem "Je n'ai pas oublié . . ."—with the denial of the work of time this opening phrase makes explicit—it becomes appropriate therefore for us to consider another short and similarly autobiographical poem, "L'Ennemi" (poem 10 of *Les Fleurs du Mal*), a sonnet dating from 1855. Although "L'Ennemi" ended up in "Spleen et Idéal" while "Je n'ai pas oublié . . ." (doubtless by virtue of its implied contrast with "la ville" of line 1) eventually became part of "Tableaux Parisiens," both poems construct a metaphorical space of habitation for the poetic self; one safe and protected with its "blanche maison" and its shabby garden, overseen by a benign and generous sun, the other, however, in the garden of a stormy youth, now devastated for lack of protection from the thunder and rain:

Voilà que j'ai touché l'automne des idées,
Et qu'il faut employer la pelle et les râteaux
Pour rassembler à neuf les terres inondées
Où l'eau creuse des trous grands comme des tombeaux.

(Already the autumn of ideas has come,
and I must dig and rake and dig again
if I am to reclaim the flooded soil
collapsing into holes the size of graves.)

What is most striking, perhaps, about this latter poem is the careful balance it creates between two different ways of experiencing time's destructiveness: if the storm of youth amounts to a single lengthy and destructive *event* ("Ma jeunesse ne fut qu'un ténébreux orage"), what, in the poet's now reflective maturity, calls into question any rehabilitation of his devastated life—the negentropic work of shovels and rakes—is the sapping of his powers that has simultaneously been occurring and is attributed to the temporal *process* of entropy that is called aging.

Time is not now manifested, then, solely as a function of a *history* the poem recounts (the event of the storm, coinciding with the subject's youth, and recognizably analogous to the devastating political events of the mid-century in Baudelaire's life). Aging has occurred also as a slow and imperceptible process by which, in parasitic fashion, growing and prospering at the expense of the life of its host, "Le Temps mange la vie" (Time consumes existence). Only the word *obscur* in line 13 ("l'obscur Ennemi qui nous ronge le coeur" [the hidden Enemy that gnaws our heart]) hints at a differentiation along these lines between the unignorably spectacular event of the storm and the imperceptible process that gradually "gnaws away" at life. But similarly, the shift from "*ma* jeunesse" to "qui *nous* ronge le coeur"—that is, from the personal and specific to the collective and general—points toward an implication that the poem's autobiographical emphasis tends to background. The work of time is twofold, and even those fortunate individuals who may escape the destructive events of history—that is, of public events—will still lose in the end to the less spectacular, more insidious, but no less destructive and absolutely certain effects of process time, the time of the everyday. And Baudelaire's personal interest embraces both, given that, different as they may be experientially (the one spectacularly damaging, the other obscurely so), they work hand in hand, and are ultimately as undissociable—so the poem's careful organization indicates—as the quatrains and tercets of a sonnet. The value of the event is as an indicator that draws attention to the underlying process, and indicates its fatal significance.

What is striking, then, is to perceive that in late Baudelaire, eventful time and everyday or process time ("eventless" time) are generally speaking treated separately. It is the resources of verse poetry that tend to be devoted to a thematics of event—of the historical and the life-changing—a thematics developed through disruptively disalienating encounters with strange and disturbing figures like the swan, the frightening *sept vieillards,* or the profoundly disturbing *passante,* And here a metaphysical dimension of modern life is implied that represents *le Mal* as a sinister *prolongement* of the supernaturalist idealism of Baudelaire's youth. Meanwhile, the poet is also beginning to experiment with prose poetry as, among other things, a poetry of the urban everyday, the site of process time—an everyday now to all intents and purposes shorn of metaphysical dimension or reference, although still regularly explored through a thematics of urban encounter.

Given the way time's two aspects are shown in "L'Ennemi" to participate jointly in a single work of destruction, one may legitimately wonder what are the stakes of Baudelaire's later assignment of event and process, transcendent and immanent understandings of time, to verse and prose respectively. My sense is that, while lacking the unifying concept of entropy, it is nevertheless a question concerning the status, not so much of time per se as of time's manifestation in the form of noise—of noise understood as constituting the atmospherics of the city, and hence the vehicle of "modern beauty"—that Baudelaire is raising. For noise raises the question of its readability: Does it signify? How does it signify? What does it signify? And it does so in a way that supports a definition of the phenomenon of disalienation as a becoming aware of the world's noisy (un) readability.

But if noise can become in this way the signifier of time that is common to Baudelaire's later verse and the prose poems he wrote contemporaneously, it is by virtue of the fact that the verse poetry of event and the prose poetry of process time share a common locus, which is the definitionally noisy city street. The street that is the site of everyday life—the street we have already seen (in chapter 2) the poet choose as an alternative to the fetish magic associated with the *vitre*—is also the place where history is made and devastating events occur: those, not only of revolution and repression, but also of urban renewal and the painful historical process (or event?) of modernization that is epitomized, in "Le Cygne," by the work of Haussmann. For the street is, again definitionally, the place where one is not at home—the place where one encounters, therefore, that which, representing the strangeness of the other, requires to be *read*. What is active both in Baudelaire's late verse and in his prose poems, therefore, is an atmosphere, one that—arising in the street—figures the disalienating semantics of the verb *to encounter*. For what one *encounters* is never the familiar, the known, the expected or the ordinary, and always that which surprises, challenges and activates a response of reading. And an encounter—as opposed to, say, a meeting—also carries a charge of sinister significance.

Modern information theory teaches that an utterance ceases to be a communicative message and becomes a readable text to the degree that noise—already present parasitically in communication—interferes in the process of its transmission and reception, blocking immediacy of understanding and constituting a form of encounter. For to become *readable* in this way is therefore to be unmasterable: there is no end to the act of reading, no point where the text becomes *known*, and the process of its reading might end. The readable is also, ultimately, the unreadable. Similarly, disalienation occurs as an awareness that the world previously experienced as familiar (in Hegel's German: *bekannt*) now resists becoming known (*erkannt*) to the precise extent that, by virtue of its now apparent noisiness, it has become strange, that is, readable.[3] The familiar, in short, has acquired an atmosphere, which endows it with interest and life to the precise extent that it excludes access to knowledge and gives rise, instead, to a sense of the object's ultimate readability (or [un]interpretability) and consequently of the subject's estrangement. The reader's alienated status in relation to a world that has become (un)readable—offering no finalities, no answers, no conclusions—is not abolished, but confirmed in the moment when the world's false familiarity falls away and its failure to be comfortably literal, its inescapably *figural* character of noisy readability, becomes evident.

Baudelaire's genius, though, shows itself in this. No single literary trope can maintain for long its defamiliarizing power to make the world strange. Repeated, it becomes familiar and thus literal; it ceases to exert the power of noise to produce readability. In offering *two* figurations of a world governed by time—as a place where (in verse) the noise of history allegorically bespeaks an evil transcending power, and as a place (in prose) where, ironically, the noise of daily process simply *exists*, in its own limitless readability—he prepares for his readers an unstable and therefore uncertain and divided position of reading, in relation to the time-governed world of the city, that mirrors the unresolvable situation of knowing that one doesn't know—the experience of an interpretability that cannot conclude—that I am calling disalienation. The two apparently irreconcilable options that are presented—time manifests itself allegorically as the transcendent power of destructive evil, but also as an absurd factor of ironic noise in the immanent relations of everyday life—place the reader in a position that recalls Friedrich Schlegel's definition of Romantic irony as "permanent parabasis."[4] One shuttles back and forth between incompatible perceptions that nevertheless together confirm and intensify, by the very fact of their irreconcilability, the sense of the world's noisy atmosphere of readability that constitutes the experience of disalienation. Literature's response to the problematics of time, experienced as the noise of entropy, is then to engineer for the reader a salutary if disconcerting experience of disalienating resistance to closure.

When, in a celebrated *fusée*, Baudelaire writes: "Deux qualités littéraires fondamentales: surnaturalism et ironie" (*OC* 1:658), we are justified, then, both in noting the apparent incompatibility of these two qualities *and* in assuming that part of the implication of the *fusée* is, nevertheless, that they are *codependent*, and understood therefore, to work bafflingly together. "Surnaturalisme," furthermore, can be understood to refer as much to Baudelaire's early practice of harmonian fetish aesthetics as to his later conversion to the allegorical (but still fetishistic) treatment of time as destructive and evil; the whole phrase ultimately provides a handy summation of Baudelaire's *oeuvre* as a whole, with its three-way tug of harmonian versus noisy supernaturalism but also of allegorical supernaturalism and ironic immanence, such that finally the conventional understanding of an *oeuvre*—as a structurally harmonious whole—is itself exploded. And in that case, my own decision to present Baudelaire's aesthetics of atmosphere in three more or less discrete but also actively interactive parts—devoted to fetishistic supernaturalism, allegorical supernaturalism, and to the prosaic ironies of an immanent everyday, respectively—finds its own support in this brief and gnomic *fusée*.

Still, the *fusée* has particular applicability, I think, to the poet's dual post-1848/51 project, in "Tableaux parisiens" and *Le Spleen de Paris*: that of exploring the essential strangeness and hence the endless readability of the city and its life—a strangeness and readability that are encapsulated in a thematics of (noisy) encounter having the street as its privileged locus. It is to that issue of encounter, in its allegorical and supernaturalist formulation, that I now turn.

Statues and Allegorical Encounter: A Stroll in the City

> L'origine de la sculpture se perd dans la nuit des temps: c'est donc un art de Caraïbes.
>
> (The origins of sculpture are lost in the dark of time: hence it is an art of savages.)
>
> *Salon de 1846* (*OC* 2:487)

> Singulier art qui s'enfonce dans les ténèbres des temps . . .
>
> (A strange art that goes back to the darkness of time . . .)
>
> *Salon de 1859* (*OC* 2:670)

It is hard to read the description of the devastated garden in "L'Ennemi" without thinking of the understanding of allegory developed by Walter Benjamin in his essay on the *Trauerspiel*: "Allegories are, in the realm of thought, what ruins are in the realm of things."[5] When we approach "Le Cygne" (poem 89), with its memorable evocation, in relation to the figures of the swan and of Andromache, of the devastation undergone by the city of Paris in the course of its modernization by Baron Haussmann, we will inevitably be led back to this Benjaminian understanding of allegory as melancholic reflection inspired by the ruins left by what has now disappeared, an *Andenken* or "penser à" (thinking toward) that is exemplified in the poem by Andromache's nostalgia, beside her "Simoïs menteur," for a Troy now lost. (See the appendix for text and translation of "Le Cygne.")

More characteristic of Baudelaire's own conception of allegory, however—although ultimately not inconsistent with Benjamin's—are the figures themselves: the displaced swan, or Andromache in exile, that are presented in the poem as occasions of encounter and objects of reflection that the poet comes across—or in vocabulary more reminiscent of "Le Soleil," stumbles upon—in the course of his urban walking. Andromache pops up in his mind ("Andromaque, je pense à vous") as he crosses "le nouveau Carrousel," and she does so in response to his also chance discovery, at an earlier time, of a stranded swan in the vicinity of a disorderly building site:

> Je ne vois qu'en esprit tout ce camp de baraques
> ....
> Là s'étalait jadis une ménagerie;
> Là je vis, un matin . . .
> ....
> Un cygne . . .

Like the "petites vieilles" of a not unrelated poem, who are described as "des êtres singuliers, décrépits et charmants," Andromache and the swan are both "monstres" and "disloqués," damaged and dislocated as they have been—both disjointed and exiled—by time in the form of history. Yet, like the poet of "L'Ennemi," they all persist—the "petites vieilles," Andromache, the swan, and all the other defeated exiles the swan poem lists—in *living on,* continuing to "chemine[r], stoïques et sans plaintes, / A travers le chaos des vivantes cités" (wander, stoic and inured / to all the uproar of the heedless town) ("Les petites vieilles," poem 91). What, then, is the relation of these "êtres singuliers" (odd creatures) to the urban chaos that surrounds them and to which they are so often directly linked? And what does it mean that their fate is not exhausted by the damage done to them, but requires also an apparently absurd, if dislocated, *Weiterleben*?

They are, of course, living ruins. "Débris d'humanité pour l'éternité mûrs" (Rubbish ready for eternity) or "Ruines! ma famille!" (Flotsam, my family!), they were once, "Les petites vieilles" insists, "des femmes, Eponine ou Laïs" (women—Laïs or Eponine), just as Andromache, now Helenus's wife, is also "veuve d'Hector." Figures of loss, then, and of a certain fallenness, they are also, and as such, victims—not so much of some blind Fate as of something much more intentional and specific, described in "Les petites vieilles" as a sinister and sadistic puppet master. As "marionnettes," then, they drag along the street; or they dance involuntarily "sans vouloir danser, pauvres sonnettes / Où se pend un Démon sans pitié" (sad doorbells / On which a merciless Devil tugs). Thus they illustrate the insight the poet had pointedly placed in the liminary poem to *Les Fleurs du Mal*, written in 1855, "Au Lecteur": "C'est le diable qui tient les fils qui nous remuent" (It's the devil who holds our puppet-strings, my translation). But the image of bells savagely tugged by a pitiless Demon adds to our awareness of a cruelty done to them, a sense also of urgency and/or alarm, as if their grotesque malformation was the sign, perhaps, of an urgent and important message to be conveyed, or as if their brokenness and angularity, their disjointedness, like that of the similarly decrepit "sept vieillards," implied some sort of warning or admonition. Is it this message carrying, then, that motivates their absurd living-on, as if it were not enough that time has broken them apart, historically, but it must also be lived out, endlessly, in a postevent everyday that, converting them from simple victims into victim messengers, makes them into figures of readability, living and walking allegories? As if history makes living people into signs of an evil cosmic or supernatural malevolence, their puppet master, while the fact of their living-on in a subsequent everyday makes that readability available, as the enigma of allegory, for those, like the poet-observer, who exist in the process time of ordinary life?

This readability is a function, in particular, of their plasticity: it is their shapedness and malleability, grotesque as it is, that betrays the work of a shaping influence, tugging on them at will. And it is in this dimensionality of shaped or misshapen *form* that the living objects of Baudelairean allegorical encounter reveal their kinship, as sculpted figures, with the many statues that one encounters in the public places of the city: its streets, squares, and gardens. Baudelaire's allegorical objects of encounter have the shaped character of statues—but more particularly of statues that have somehow come alive and are able to move. As such they are uncanny figures whose mobility the poems often dwell upon, noting especially its *impeded* character, as in the gait, not only of the "petites vieilles," but also of the "sept vieillards" with their "pas maladroit / D'un quadrupède infirme ou d'un Juif à trois pattes" (clumsy gait of some lame animal or three-legged Jew), and most particularly of the lost swan, "de ses pieds palmés frottant le pavé sec" (with its webbed feet clumsy on the cobblestones), and of its human equivalent, the "négresse phtisique" (consumptive negress) shuffling, haggard of eye, in the snow.

But they are uncanny too because, like the *vieillards* as they advance "vers un but inconnu" (toward an unknown goal), they seem, simultaneously and contradictorily, charged with a mission—one whose intended recipient is none other than the observing poet himself, who may well write, on occasion, "Là je vis . . . / un cygne" (There I saw a swan), as if the encounter were a matter of pure chance, but who also writes: "Tout à coup, un vieillard . . . / M'apparut" (Suddenly an old man . . . appeared to me, my translation), signaling in this way his sense of being singled out as the *destinataire* of some sort of annunciation—a privilege he understands, at best, imperfectly. "À une passante" is, of course, the classic case of this strange amalgam of the certainty of being directly targeted by a statue-like moving figure ("Moi je buvais, . . . / Dans son oeil, . . . / La douceur qui fascine et le plaisir qui tue" [I drank from her eyes . . . the grace that beckons and the joy that kills]) with an equally strong sense of disorientation and uncertainty: "Car j'ignore où tu fuis, tu ne sais où je vais" (Of me you know nothing, I nothing of you). And *this* figure's "jambe de statue" (line 5; statuesque leg, my translation), which *may* be revealed quite inadvertently, but may *also* be coquettishly displayed—the formulation "avec sa jambe de statue" implies only that her leg is visible—captures something like the essence of Baudelaire's definitionally uncertain understanding of allegorical manifestations of all kinds, as they occur in the life of the city as objects of encounter. Arising in apparently aleatory circumstances, they seem nevertheless to be purposive and to have a message or meaning to deliver, even though that message's content, and even its destination, are themselves uncertain as well. And, like the *passante*—herself a figure of time and specifically of history, as we will see in chapter 4—they exert the charged combination of attraction and guilt that betrays an association with sexuality, that other thinly veiled but insistent, atmospheric presence that makes the urban environment electric.

This crucial ambivalence or uncertainty of the statuesque and the allegorical, the sexual and the cosmic, is registered, finally, in a striking coincidence, across virtually the full span of Baudelaire's creative career, of two hemistichs that each relate to the (non)display of female lower limbs. "Avec sa jambe de statue" in "A une passante" echoes, and simultaneously rewrites, "cachant leurs membres nus" (hiding their naked limbs) in "Je n'ai pas oublié . . . ."[6] In condensed form, this pairing of two hemistichs can stand, then, for the dynamics of occultation and revelation—of time denied and time acknowledged—that defines the terms of Baudelaire's historical evolution (where *time,* of course, implies also distance or extension, difference, and ultimately noise). But the *same* dynamics of denial and acknowledgement are active also in the continued and unresolved ambivalence about time and its entailments that can still be perceived in the poet's late writing, and specifically in the baffled or at least mixed feeling, the sense of estrangement, that he brings to his perception of the everyday as a locus of the uncanny, and consequently also to his understanding of allegory in relation to the atmospherics of the noisy city. So it is not surprising that such feelings surface, finally, whenever—as in the *Salons* of 1846 and 1859—he is led to write essayistically about sculpture and sculptural form, and to do the theory, so to speak, of the statuesque.[7]

For in that writing too it is the shapedness and dimensionality of statues—along with the primordial and indeed primitive character that, for him, betrays their relation to time—that interests and simultaneously disturbs him, requiring theorization. It is not accidental that, already in "Je n'ai pas oublié . . ., " the "Pomone de plâtre" and the "vieille Vénus" (note the adjective), represent—with their concealed limbs—ancient, pre-Christian, and female divinities, and that they do so by contrast with a male god of light functioning currently and who supplants them: the sun whose generosity, aided by the *vitre* of art, cancels the frugality and mediocrity of the middle-class world, with its "nappe frugale" and its "rideaux de serge," and does so by means of a device akin not to sculpture but to painting, and productive of what I called a "nappe de lumière" (with its "reflets de cierge" that strongly suggest Catholicism). This poem implicitly writes a *history,* and a history of progress, even as it seeks—fetishistically and as a matter of "artificial supernaturalism"—to counter the effect of time. Small wonder, then, that time thus repressed was destined to return, although not before history had again been mobilized, in the *Salon de 1846*, against the association of statuary with time.

Indeed we can measure the degree to which the young Baudelaire experienced sculpture as a threat to the fetishizing aesthetics of artificial or idealizing supernaturalism by noticing the intensity with which, in "Pourquoi la sculpture est ennuyeuse," he seeks to reject it, as a survival of the archaic and the primitive: an "art de Caraïbe" and a fetish in the only sense of that word then current, that of a primitive, ugly, and hopelessly irrational religious idol.

> *L'origine de la sculpture se perd dans la nuit des temps*: c'est donc un art de Caraïbes. En effet, nous voyons tous les peuples tailler fort adroitement des fétiches avant d'aborder la peinture, qui est un art de raisonnement profond . . . etc.
>
> (*The origins of sculpture are lost in the darkness of time*: hence it is an art of savages. And indeed all peoples can be seen to sculpt skillful fetish figures before they turn to painting, which is an art of profound reasoning . . . etc.)
>
> (*OC* 2:487)[8]

Needless to say, the sign of sculpture's primitive status is none other than its shapedness and three-dimensionality, which is read here, not yet as evidence of an allegorical structure of thought, but as proof of sculpture's boring because naïve naturalism. "La sculpture se rapproche de la nature" (Sculpture lies close to nature); "Brutale et positive comme la nature, elle est en même temps vague et insaisissable, parce qu'elle montre trop de faces à la fois" (Like nature brutal and positive, it is simultaneously vague and baffling, because it displays too many aspects at once). Sculpture, therefore, cannot impose a viewing perspective on the spectator, as the artifice of painting does: "Le spectateur, qui tourne autour de la figure, peut choisir cent points de vue différents, excepté le bon" (The viewer, turning about the figure, can choose a hundred different points of view other than the correct one). And, worst of all, a purely accidental circumstance may reveal some sort of beauty in a statue that, disconcertingly, the sculptor had not intended: "C'est pourquoi il est aussi difficile de se connaître en sculpture que d'en faire de mauvaise" (Hence it is as difficult to master sculpture as it is to produce a bad statue). The statue is a noisy phenomenon in that, prefiguring as it does the Freudian unconscious, it defies the rational mind, the advanced intelligence, of 1840s modernity.

It is possible, however, that this last comment ("difficile de s'y connaître") gives away the game. Coming as it does at the culmination of a suspiciously spirited diatribe, it unintentionally reveals what it actually is that the young Baudelaire finds so "ennuyeuse"—that is, not simply boring, but also, in another sense of the word, annoying and troublesome—about sculpture. This would be the very feature of baffling and bothersome strangeness—the atmospherics—that by 1859 will have become, in a typically Baudelairean reversal, the entirely positive indicator of sculpture's allegorical character of readability. If it is "difficile de se connaître en sculpture," *that* will be the very reason why, still experiencing sculpture as disconcerting and disturbing, the later Baudelaire finds in the statue, as a fetish figure and an "art de Caraïbe," a model of practice for a certain, fundamentally revised, art of poetry—one that, like sculpture, now *requires* movement of its readers, rather than imposing on them a single, privileged perspective, and does so by shifting the ground, as it were, from beneath their feet, so that—to put it mildly—it becomes "difficile de s'y connaître." A poetry whose modernity lies, now, not in its rationality, but in its strange and elusive, but also suggestive art of infinite readability, offering as it does—like the strangeness of the everyday urban world—innumerable points of access without discernibly hierarchizing them, let alone imposing a single perspective.

So it is now by virtue of its relation to time, as a primordial figure and an art "qui se perd dans la nuit des temps"—by virtue, that is, of its noisily interpretable dimensionality and shapedness—that sculpture acquires a crucial function in the modern age: that of figuring, for moderns who have become so out of touch with the real nature of the world, the sinister power of Time as the unseen Enemy of human life, working as it does through the storms of history, but also as the unperceived parasite that prospers by consuming our lives. It turns out then, in 1859, that "devant un objet tiré de la nature et représenté par la sculpture, c'est-à-dire rond, fuyant, autour duquel on peut tourner librement, et comme l'objet naturel lui-même, environné d'atmosphère" (*OC* 2:671; in the presence of an object drawn from nature and represented by sculpture, that is, round, elusive, around which one can turn freely, and like the natural object itself surrounded by atmosphere), the peasant, the savage, "l'homme primitif," have an incomparable advantage over moderns in the form of access to a knowledge and a truth from which the latter can only profit. For if, in 1846, Baudelaire had espoused the doctrine of aesthetic progress for the purpose of reviling the power of statuary, he is now inclined to subscribe to precisely the opposite view: "Le bas-relief est déjà un mensonge, c'est-à-dire un pas fait vers un art plus civilisé, s'éloignant autant de l'idée pure de sculpture" (*OC* 2:671; already a bas-relief is a lie, a step in the direction of a more civilized art, and one that accordingly departs to the same extent from the pure idea of sculpture). Pomona and Venus are rehabilitated; the doctrine of progress, espoused in the utopian 1840s but having been adopted in the interim by the Second Empire for purposes of its own, is no longer tenable. And an archaic art, one that, by virtue of its very age as well as of the dimensionality, the readability that is the sign of that age, bespeaks time and enforces movement—a necessary change of perspective—has become of crucial significance to moderns. And that is because, in becoming "civilized," they have fallen into illusion, blindness, and error.

For it is as signifiers of Time and inscrutable bearers of atmosphere that statues *haunt* the modern city, like so much noise in the environment. If they seem likely to come alive at any moment—ready to walk—it is in uncanny compensation for the modern disinclination to budge from the narrow, alienated perspective that ignores the noise of existence, and as bearers, therefore, of the disalienated and disalienating message that we are the creatures, and the victims, of Time in its various unheeded manifestations. Meanwhile, *we* can turn about *them*, walking now ourselves, in hopes of glimpsing some hint of the shattering, because enlightening, perspective to which, by virtue of their allegorical readability, they wordlessly allude. For the language of statues is not speech but gesture; and allegory is the figure that makes speech itself gestural, endowing it with an indexical function, in the way that a statue too may describe or represent, but does so in order to indicate or allude.

By way of introducing his discussion of two allegorical statues by Ernest Christophe that were *not* exhibited at the 1859 Salon, Baudelaire begins by taking his readers on a statue-by-statue stroll through the city that amounts to a catalogue of recognized allegorical types together with the conventional urban setting that forms their habitat: libraries for Harpocrates, Apollo, and the Muses; a shrubbery or *bosquet*, of course, for Melancholia; churches and cemeteries for memorial statues and figures of grief; public gardens for Venus and Hebe; pompous city squares and intersections for legendary figures of glory, war, knowledge or martyrdom. Baudelaire's intent is to contrast the trivial works submitted to the Salon with what he views as sculpture's sacred function, "le rôle divin de la sculpture" (*OC* 2:670): the strange pregnancy with otherworldly significance that it derives from its allegorical character. Most of these typical figures are caught, then, in the act of a signifying gesture: "Harpocrate, un doigt posé sur la bouche, vous commande le silence" (*OC* 2:669–70; Harpocrates, with a finger to his lips, commands your silence); Melancholia's gesture consists in her very stillness, as she "mire son visage auguste dans les eaux d'un bassin" (mirrors her august countenance in the waters of a pond); a skeletal corpse "soulève discrètement l'énorme couvercle de son sépulcre" (discreetly lifts the huge cover of its sepulchre); Mourning lies prostrate, "échevelée, noyée dans le ruisseau de ses larmes" (her hair awry, drowning in the stream of her tears); the love goddesses, of course, "étalent . . . les rondeurs de leurs membres charmants" (show off their charmingly rounded limbs), while famous men hold emblematic objects and may point to heaven "où ils ont sans cesse aspiré" (to which they have ceaselessly aspired), or else "désignent le sol d'où ils se sont élévés" (point to the ground from which they have risen). The injunctions, intimations, exhortations, or commands of all these gesturing figures are couched, then, in the somewhat uncanny "langage muet" (silent speech) of action strangely stilled, the frozen gesture.

And that is why, in the propitious semidarkness of libraries or chapels, the shaded verdure of shrubberies, gardens and cemeteries, the pompous solemnity of city squares and the like, sculptured representations of gesture can so readily suggest to the sensitive passerby that the statue is caught in the act of returning to life, as the skeletal corpse emerging from its tomb is so incontrovertibly doing. And also—most compellingly of all—as does the statue of the appropriately named Commendatore in the Don Juan myth, memorably brought to the stage in Mozart's *Don Giovanni*:

> Fussiez-vous le plus insoucieux des hommes, le plus malheureux ou le plus vil, le fantôme de pierre s'empare de vous pendant quelques minutes, et vous *commande*, au nom du passé, de penser aux choses qui ne sont pas de la terre.
>
> Tel est le rôle divin de la sculpture.
>
> (Were you the most carefree of humans, the most miserable or the most vile, the stone ghost takes hold of you for a time, and *commands* you, in the name of the past, to think of things not of this earth.
>
> Such is sculpture's divine role.)
>
> (*OC* 2:670; my italics)

But notice here Baudelaire's unobtrusive modification of the myth. The traditional Commendatore returns in the name of Heaven: Baudelaire's figure walks in the name of the past, and thus as an envoy of Time. The stone guest, moreover, has become a stone ghost, a "fantôme de pierre," and more like a spectral envoy of the underworld, to which he dispatches Giovanni, than of the celestial kingdom. And the fleetingness of the sense of an unholy if divine visitation ("pendant quelques minutes") does not diminish the impression so much as it renders it more dubious, more uncanny than a heavenly annunciation is thought to be.

It matters, then, that—along with the variant of "rêve sculptural" (sculptural dream)—the word *fantôme* (ghost) has twice before been used of statues, in a space of less than two pages. Such insistence drives home this idea of sculpture's fulfilling a "divine" role on earth. The hushing figure in the library is a "fantôme impérieux" (imperious ghost), and the skeletal corpse emerging from the tomb is a "fantôme décharné" (fleshless ghost); so that it is as if, by virtue of a submerged pun (*décharnement* suggesting *acharnement*), the *imperiousness* of the sculptural injunction were proportional to the degree of immateriality, of *décharnement*, achieved by the hardness of stone, making the statue a kind of oxymoron. The "rêve sculptural," the "fantôme de pierre" paradoxically makes use of ordinary matter in order to assert a spiritual idea. Commanding us, then, by means of sculptured stone, to think of things that are not of the earth, it is in this way an agent of Baudelairean allegory—and allegory, in turn, has in Baudelaire's understanding the ghostly power of sculpture, *haunting* the living—that is, *inhabiting* our world as part of our everyday but doing so as it were *frequentatively* and hence insistently, with the special emphasis of matter inspirited, the divine bodied forth, made (sculptured) flesh, or *chair*. (Baudelaire here is very close to anticipating Freud's interest in the kinship of the familiar and the strange, the known and the unknown, the *heimlich* and the *unheimlich*.[9])

Statues, then, are matter come fleetingly to life in order to enjoin attention to eternity, even as they continue to dwell among us, as part of the everyday world to which, ordinarily, we pay so little heed. As such, they constitute a "singulier art" (peculiar art) indeed, one that, in two senses, plunges, or as Baudelaire says, "s'enfonce dans les ténèbres du temps" (thrusts down into the darkness of time): they are archaic, but also they recede from the here and now into eternity, the darkness of time of which, in their "langage muet" (mute speech) of gesture, they speak. And their function, then, as Baudelaire says of the statue of Harpocrates at the outset, is in this way Pythagorean and pedagogical. Their gesture, or better their *gestus*—that is, the impact they have on us, the action they exert—is, as befits a numinous, mysterious teacher, "plein d'autorité" (well endowed with authority). This understanding of the strange, allegorical power of statues is both fully compatible with everything that is said of sculpture's troublesomeness in the 1846 *Salon*, and an exact reversal of the theory laid out there of what is so boring about it. It is because it is "ennuyeuse" in both senses that it is difficult indeed to "s'y connaître" (to master it).

For finally, the statue, we learn, is a "fantôme immobile" (*OC* 2:671; motionless ghost), but one that solemnizes everything, "même le mouvement" (even movement), in the way that lyric poetry ennobles everything, "même la, passion" (even passion). This fourth and final recurrence of the word *fantôme* seems intended to resume the mystery of sculpture in a final paradox, one that suggests that what is phantasmal about statues is their ability to endow distance, extension, difference and their entailment of noise (summed up here as the "movement" that these entail) with the solemnity associated with stillness. In the way that they reconcile the everyday and the eternal, the material and the immaterial, the reassuring and the troubling, then, statues "donne[nt] à tout ce qui est humain quelque chose d'éternel et qui participe de la dureté de la matière employée" (*OC* 2:671; endow all that is human with something timeless that participates of the hardness of the matter it employs), an immunity from the effects of temporality. They reconcile the dignity of mobility with the indignity of the immobile, then. But they do so in the way that rhyme, as the principle of lyric poetry, "ennoblit tout, même la passion" (ennobles all, even passion)—that is, under the sole condition of submitting to the inevitability of distance, which implies movement, in its reliance on the extension represented by the line of verse. Movement, then, in Baudelaire's thinking, is the condition of the "rêve sculptural" in the way that verse is the condition of rhyme; and we will see that Baudelaire's verse allegories reference the cosmic rhyming they assume as their metaphysical framework by means of the figure of the imperfect chiasmus: a form of noisy, because extended, rhyme.

Meanwhile, it is the "rhyming" character of statues, their twofold composition manifested under the condition of movement, that accounts for Baudelaire's passionate endorsement of two allegorical statues by Ernest Christophe that he now deploys—despite the fact that Christophe had not exhibited that year—as the culminating moment of his argument concerning sculpture in the 1859 *Salon.* He had earlier rendered them into verse, as "Le Masque" (poem 20) and "Danse macabre" (poem 92, incorporated into "Tableaux Parisiens" in 1861). The first of these figures exploits sculpture's dimensionality by presenting a front and a back. "Vue de face" (from the front), it represents "un visage souriant et mignard, un visage de théâtre" (a smiling, appealing face, a theatrical face). But, "en faisant un pas de plus à gauche ou à droite, vous découvrez le secret de l'allégorie, . . . je veux dire la véritable tête révulsée, se pâmant dans les larmes et l'agonie" (*OC* 2:678; stepping a little more to the left or right, you perceive the allegory's secret, . . . I mean the real head thrown back in a faint of tears and death agony). The second is a figurine representing "un grand squelette feminin tout prêt à partir pour la fête" a tall woman's skeleton dressed to leave for a party, her eyes indistinguishably seeking "dans l'espace l'heure délicieuse du rendez-vous ou l'heure solennelle du sabbat inscrit au cadran invisible des siècles" (the delicious hour of a lovers' meeting or the solemn hour of the witches' sabbath written on the invisible clockface of the centuries), and "toute cette pensée funèbre se dress[ant] sur le piédestal d'une fastueuse crinoline" (*OC* 2:679; this whole funereal idea supported on the pedestal of a magnificent crinoline). This time it is for the statue to move forward, toward the spectator: "O charme du néant follement attifé" (O lure of nothingness so well tricked out), Baudelaire had written in "Danse macabre" and now repeats:

> Viens-tu troubler avec ta puissante grimace,
> La fête de la vie?

> (Are you planning to disturb the feast of life with the power of your ugly leer?)
>
> (lines 21–22)

If we take these two Christophe poems together, then, it seems that, as figures of allegory, statues require of the observer a complex act of reading—one that, exactly like an appreciation of rhyme, entails a double movement in time, simultaneously forward and backward. One must see beyond the illusory present to the ugly truth of a distant past (represented, as in "Le Masque," by the figure of death), but one must also measure, as "Danse macabre" proposes, the continued impact of that remote past as it impinges on the present, the pressure that it exerts on the here and now. Baudelaire's figure for this "rhyming" effect of allegory, with the double dynamic of convergence-divergence within time, is chiasmus: and chiasmic reading, I suggest, is one of the possible implications of the word *contortions* as it occurs in the final stanza—not quoted in the *Salon*—of "Danse macabre":

> En tout climat, sous tout soleil, la Mort t'admire
> En tes contorsions, risible Humanité,
> Et souvent, comme toi, se parfumant de myrrhe,
> Mêle son ironie à ton insanité!
>
> (Death in every latitude dotes on you
> and your contortions, ludicrous Humanity,
> and often, like you, daubing herself with myrrh,
> mixes her scorn with your delirium.)
>
> (lines 56–60)

To read an allegory, in other words—submitting to the "contorsion" its back-and-forth, convergent-divergent dynamic imposes—is to experience the irony that is the presence of Death amid the frivolity and general *inconscience* of life. An irony that in turn we will see represented, not only in "Le Cygne," but also in "Les sept vieillards" and "À une passante" (see chapter 4), as arising at the crossing point of a chiasmic *X*; so that allegory emerges as an atmospheric space-between of spectrality constituted by the rhyming relation of past and present, but centered on an encounter with death in life. This is the encounter of which Don Giovanni's rendezvous with the statue of the Commendatore is emblematic.

And it is such an encounter, I submit, that is produced by what I want to show to be the chiasmic patterning of "Le Cygne," by which I mean the contortions, not unlike the swan's own writhing beneath a "ciel ironique et cruellement bleu," that one must perform as the swan poem proceeds, moving backward and forward at the same time. For "Le Cygne," as we will see, is a poem about allegory that also enacts, in the structure of its first part, allegory's own x-like structure of temporal divergence and convergence. But it is also, and likewise, a poem about the cause-and-effect relation of allegory to melancholy, and one that simultaneously reverses that relation, implicit in the positioning of parts 1 and 2, into another chiasmus. For if allegorical perception as cause induces the mood of melancholy as its effect, it is also true that melancholy in turn predisposes one to an allegorical view of existence, thus reversing their relations. The pensiveness of the poem's mood, therefore, is not just a matter of thought, but rather an effect of the kind of thinking, compounded both of allegory and melancholy, that is an inclusive *penser à*, in that it is directed toward an ultimate object that thought cannot actually attain. This is the thought—exemplified by the apostrophe: "Andromaque, je pense à vous!"—that cannot extend all the way back, beyond humanity's fall into time, to the evil eternity that, for Baudelaire, controls our fallen existence. For apostrophe is a figure of address, implying communication, but of address to that which lies beyond the normal condition of communication that is the presence of a true addressee.

Such apostrophe-like pensiveness is the "thinking-toward" that Walter Benjamin refers to by employing the word *Andenken*: not simply the pensiveness of melancholy, but the melancholy of allegorical awareness. Baudelaire's word for it, though, would be rather something like reflection, or perhaps reflectivity, since for him the ultimate model of such thought, like the relation of Andromache to the swan and of the swan to Andromache, is the play of reflections, the "jeu de reflets" that is rhyme: rhyme with whose hazardousness—its subjection to, and affinity with, noise—"Le soleil" has already acquainted us (cf. chapter 2). Allegorical rhyming is a chiasmic structure of encounter that forms an atmospheric "jeu de reflets"; but that atmosphere is itself an *apo-strophein* that turns toward—turns its reader toward—an *ultimate* object of thought that lies beyond human ken. Its sign, therefore, is the *X* of mystery—the mystery of "subliminality."

History, Disalienation, and Urban Atmospherics: "Le Cygne"

> Au détour d'un bosquet, abritée sous de lourds ombrages, l'éternelle Mélancolie mire son visage auguste dans les eaux d'un bassin, immobile comme elle. Et le rêveur qui passe, attristé et charmé, contemplant cette grande figure aux membres robustes, mais alanguis par une peine secrète, dit: Voilà ma sœur!
>
> (Behind a clump of trees, sheltered by dense shade, eternal Melancholy reflects her noble face in the waters of a pond that is as still as she. And the passing dreamer, both saddened and enchanted, says as he contemplates this tall figure whose strong limbs droop from a secret sadness: she is my sister!)
>
> *Salon de 1859* (OC 2:669)

> Paris change! mais rien dans ma mélancolie
> N'a bougé! palais neufs, échafaudages, blocs,
> Vieux faubourgs, tout pour moi devient allégorie!
> Et mes chers souvenirs sont plus lourds que des rocs.
>
> "Le Cygne" (lines 29–32)

The rhyming cities of modern Paris and ancient Troy in "Le Cygne" are sites where the destructive force of time, in the guise of the events of history, produces figures that likewise rhyme allegorically—the swan and Andromache, figures whose melancholic living-on in a state of disalienation makes of them strangely disturbing "statues." For, rather than representing a state of stillness in the act of coming to life, they reverse this relation, and seem to be living creatures stilled into near immobility by the fate that life has inflicted on them, their exile, as well as by the very reflectiveness that *defines* their exile from, and within, life. *Reflectiveness* here means both the reflective thought, the melancholy into which they are plunged in their state of disalienation, and the way their fates reflect each other allegorically, so that the poet, passing by, might well say of each "Voilà ma soeur!" *Reflection* refers to thought, and also to a mode of resemblance.

Reflection in both senses also implies distance and mediation, a *penser à,* so it is significant that the mediating figure implied here, between the swan and Andromache, is that of Aeneas, the traveler. It is *his* report of Andromache, in the *Aeneid,* that the poem references, and the turbulent history of Rome, therefore, that connects the sack of Troy with the destructive modernization of Paris, triangulating in this way the dual relations of the swan and Andromache, Paris and Troy, in the way that a line of verse provides the necessary mediation of poetic rhyme, or in the way that "tout *pour moi* devient allégorie" (my emphasis). For the poet too crossing "le nouveau Carrousel" (line 6) is like Aeneas traversing provincial Greece between Asia Minor and Italy; and it is in his mind that the triangulation occurs that invokes the *Aeneid* in response to the riddle of the swan: "Andromaque, je pense à vous!" For this reason, however, the allegorizing modern poet, with his stranded swan, is in an epigonic or imitative relation to the epic hero whom he rhymes with—a hero, however, who as a version of Ulysses is himself an imitator—as well as with that hero's likewise epigonic Roman poet, Virgil, Rome being, in matters aesthetic and philosophical, deeply indebted to Athens. And this relation of late epigon to early epigon is, furthermore, not at all unlike that of the poor stranded swan—a bedraggled "mythe étrange et fatal" (line 24)—in relation to the once noble Andromache who has fallen in Greece from her erstwhile mythic greatness: "Veuve d'Hector, hélas! et femme d'Hélenus" (line 40).

Each of the two moderns, the swan and the poet, is a rhyme figure, then, but one even baser than their somewhat nobler, albeit already tarnished, partners-in-rhyme, be they Virgil or Andromache. In its westward-moving history (Troy-[Athens]-Rome-Paris), urban civilization cannot be said, in the world of the poem, to have experienced that history as progress, in the way that the culture of the positivist Second Empire liked to insist. Rather it has been a matter of regress, the institution of civilization itself having constituted, it seems, the original fall from grace in relation to nature and qualifying, therefore, as the prime mover of history's long, and still ongoing decline, from the already slightly tarnished sublimity of Troy to the pathetic inanity of the swan, "avec ses gestes fous,"—"Comme les exilés, ridicule et sublime / Et rongé d'un désir sans trêve!" (lines 34–36)—the swan which, in that respect, is also akin to Paris's (similarly spastic) *petites vieilles*, who likewise doggedly live on in the grip of their own cruel puppet master.

In countering in this way Second Empire ideology concerning the supposedly upward direction of history, the poem simultaneously confirms Baudelaire's own volte-face, à propos of sculpture, on the issue of aesthetic progress. The dynamics of rhyme no longer functions, for him, amelioratively, as it once did, countering the disenchanting movement of history by ennobling the ordinary in conformity with a fetishizing aesthetics of the ideal. It functions now as an agent of that disenchantment. By espousing historical decline, moving as it does from the sublime in the direction of the ridiculous, it forms in the interim an amalgam of the two, like the swan—a state that thus indexes exile as a situation of disalienation in the mode of melancholic reflection. And allegory, the correspondingly exilic trope, becomes a *penser à* or *Andenken* that, therefore, looks nostalgically backward, toward a nobler past, and in the opposite direction from the movement of rhyme.

But allegory's rhyming of the fallen present with the less tarnished past is also directed toward an imagined origin, the fall out of eternity into history—an origin understood as both the cause of history's long decline and a source lost to human retrieval. The objects that allegorical thought encounters in the past are more noble than contemporary figures but nevertheless, and simultaneously, already in decline and irretrievably tarnished because always already historical. As such, though, they bear witness to an even more ancient disaster, in the way that Andromache in Greece refers us to the fall of Troy. So, like sculpture, allegory plunges—"s'enfonce" is Baudelaire's more active verb—into "les ténèbres du temps," but its function is to *haunt the present*, through the witness it bears in that way to the ancient, and disastrous, originary fall out of eternity and into history. Thus it inspires melancholic disalienation as an *insight without knowledge*, given that real knowledge of that ultimate and primary object cannot be attained. It is as if between us and it stretches a hazy atmosphere, the domain of allegory, an atmosphere made of the noisy rhyming of present-day figures with figures from the historical past, but serving both to uncover the existence of, and to conceal from sight, the transcendent force, outside of time, that is responsible for all the devastation, exile, and pain: *le Mal.* The fact of history is forced in this way on our otherwise unwilling attention, inspiring melancholic brooding in the face of its absurdity and impenetrability.

It is in light of an analysis such as this that the curious narrative structuring of part 1 of "Le Cygne" merits attention. It requires us, as we read, to follow the declining direction of history, as the narrative as narration moves forward, from the narrator's thinking of (or about) Andromache to his previous encounter with the swan, which supplies the explanatory context for his interest in Andromache. Simultaneously, we must reconstruct from that narration a narrated story—one that, conversely, *begins* with the enigma of the swan and moves back to the idea of Andromache as the swan puzzle's resolution, having recourse to the retrospective movement of thought that is allegory. The crisscross of forward-moving narration and backward-looking narrated forms a mental chiasmus, which might be formulated as "Andromache (in the narration) is to the swan what the swan (in the narrated) is to Andromache," the forward direction of history and the retrospective thinking of allegory, its recourse to memory, being rendered compatible by the participation of each in time.

Between the two figures, then, stretches—still in the readers' minds—a between-space of mutual reflection, the space whose "jeu de reflets" is centered, as it were, on the crossing point of the chiasmic X. It is a noisy space of transition or *traversée,* in which the narrator, having thought of Andromache while himself crossing "le nouveau Carrousel," is now understood to be ambling—both mentally and physically, in space and in memory—through the "vieux" Paris of the old Doyenné neighborhood that, in 1859, no longer existed as an actual neighborhood, its clutter of old houses having been recently swept away by Haussman's modernization of the city.[10] The poem's *I* reflects, then, on the pain of historical change: "Le vieux Paris n'est plus (la forme d'une ville / Change plus vite, hélas, que le cœur d'un mortel)" (lines 7–8); then he recalls, more specifically (in "Je ne vois qu'en esprit . . ."), the messy *chantier*—ruins of the vanished past already pointing toward "le nouveau Paris"—where, at some time before his thinking of Andromache, he had come upon the strange figure of the stranded swan. And thus the junction of the two figures is brought about: their chiasmic meeting has required a transition through time that is mimicked by the poet's traversal of spatial extension.

But in quatrain four of the seven-quatrain section—that is, at the exact point of chiasmic crossover—what we read is this:

> Là s'étalait jadis une ménagerie;
> Là je vis, un matin, à l'heure où sous les cieux
> Froids et clairs le Travail s'éveille, où la voirie
> Pousse un sombre ouragan dans l'air silencieux,
>
> Un cygne . . .
>
> (lines 13–17)

What follows is the three-quatrain description of the stranded swan that exactly balances the three opening quatrains, governed as they are by Andromache and her "douleurs de veuve," the nostalgic melancholy that in turn triggers the narrator's similarly nostalgic reflection on the life of cities in time. And it is these thoughts that themselves connect, thanks to his "mémoire fertile," and as if by rhyme, the swan's situation "près d'un ruisseau sans eau" with the Trojan exile beside her own artificial river, her "Simoïs menteur." So the bleakness of the urban dawn scene of lines 13–17 with its "cieux / froids et clairs" seems a slightly alien interpolation—until one reflects that the swan, unlike Andromache but somewhat like the narrator, is pictured in turn imploring "le ciel ironique et cruellement bleu" (line 26). The earlier mention of a remote and uncaring sky links the stranded bird, then, to a city scene that has no equivalent in Andromache's plight: the "awakening" of the workers and the "sombre ouragan" of the street cleaners at work in the streets at dawn. The allusion, under the Empire, is necessarily oblique, but it is unmistakable. It references the tempest of history—the word *ouragan* will recur in "À une passante"—that awakened the Paris workers only to leave them high and dry in 1848: the uprisings or *descentes dans la rue* of February, then June, with the bloodbath that marked the eventual abandonment of the working class by the property-owning class, ensuring—as it turned out—the takeover of the revolution by Bonapartist imperialism. (The Place du Carrousel had been the site of a notably egregious massacre.)

At the section's crossing point, where the two branches of the historical/allegorical chiasmus meet amid the disorder of the building site, the roar of the *voirie* and the noisy *réveil* of labor, we encounter a glimpse, then, only lightly veiled, of horror, of history's devastating power of destruction. But the clear and cold sky also poses another question: that of an apparently empty site of transcendence, and of the abyss that, in Baudelaire's vision, lies beyond historical time itself. Is this inscrutable heaven occupied by a cruel and evil power that controls humanity's puppet strings? If so, that power is not in evidence here, and the cold, clear heavens are at best a site of irony: the figure that stages a subject whose presence in discourse is detectable only as a teasingly imperceptible hint or trace.

The alternative conclusion, then, is that the sky is clear, cold, and *empty*; that the very idea of transcendence is itself, therefore, null and void. We see here why it might be that, if allegory is the figural mode of Baudelaire's late verse, the function of disalienation is transferred in the prose poems to irony, as the marker of an inscrutable, and indeed apparently "absent," cosmic subject. It is also apparent that such agnosticism concerning the existence and nature of transcendence is itself a modern phenomenon, and a function of the downstream situation, in relation to the flow of time, of the swan, of the city workers, and of course, of Baudelaire himself, all of whom, unlike Andromache, must face a "ciel ironique et cruellement bleu" (see chapter 5). Closer to the source, ancient Andromache is untroubled by such issues, so that ultimately allegory, with its backward-looking perspective, begins to appear, in its Baudelairean guise, as itself a characteristically *modern* response to supernaturalist dubiety. If the swan has its *répondant* in the earlier figure of Andromache, the same is not true of Andromache herself. So the noisy atmosphere of chiasmatic reflectivity and rhyming that allegory creates, its melancholy "jeu de reflets," functions as the ambiguously readable sign of a transcendence, cruel, ironic and *now* lost to direct knowledge—but a transcendence, nevertheless, and one that once was and still, therefore, may be.

What awaits the reader, in any case, at the chiasmic crossing point, is a glimpse of horror, "un éclair . . . puis la nuit!" to cite "À une passante" and its telling recourse, in those suspension points, to the hint of spectrality contained in the figure of preterition. So it is notable that if "Le Cygne" rhymes its part 1, concerned with allegory, with a part 2 that both describes and enacts the response to allegorical insight that is melancholic disalienation, the poem as a whole also proposes a second mental chiasmus, one that crosses in the space that separates the two parts. The order of the rhyme words "mélancolie" and "allégorie," as they occur in the opening quatrain of the second part (lines 29 and 31), inverts the order in which the themes of allegory and melancholy are enacted in the overall structure of the poem:

> Paris change! mais rien dans ma mélancolie
> N'a bougé! palais neufs, échafaudages, blocs,
> Vieux faubourgs, tout pour moi devient allégorie,
> Et mes chers souvenirs sont plus lourds que des rocs.

(And "blocs" / "rocs," by the way, anticipates the inverted rhyme of "cor" / "encor" in the final quatrain, where also "s'exile" / "île" inverts the final syllable of "mélancolie."[11]) So the crisscross of narrative chiasmus that is enacted in the mind of the reader of part 1 is reproduced now in relation to the erratic relation of allegory and melancholy, melancholy and allegory—each apparently generating the other—that is enacted in the poem as a whole.

We might say, then, that the poem is not so much *about* allegory and melancholy per se, as it makes use of their relation of mutual reflectivity for the purpose of producing in the reader's mind an *atmosphere of reflection,* chiasmic in character, at the heart of which she or he may glimpse an object of encounter beyond verbal formulation: the specter of a transcendence. Baudelaire might parse that transcendence here as that of absolute evil, *le Mal;* but I would want to speak too of the painful "beauty" of modernity—something like what he describes in the opening paragraphs of *Le Peintre de la vie moderne* as beauty's absolute, whose vehicle is the relative beauty of the age (*OC* 2:685–86). By virtue of its very emptiness, the blank space that separates parts 1 and 2 of "Le Cygne" would be the sign—the *cygne*—of that absent visionary object, so that it is as if the chiasmic structure of Baudelairean allegory functioned, in the end, somewhat in the manner of the explicit form of classical allegory in which, for example, a blindfolded woman "represents" materially the abstraction that is the idea of Justice.

Just so, the *X* of a chiasmus crosses at its center point, but opens, in every direction, onto a surrounding void.[12]

FOUR

Daylight Specters: Allegory and the Weather of Time

The chiasmic figure of allegory plunges, statue-like, into the darkest night of time, as we have seen. But it can also represent—without contradiction—a spatial configuration: that of a world conceived as an X-like site of conjunction, opening in one direction onto the everyday but stretching in the other toward infinity. Disalienating encounters can thus occur, in everyday life, with figures of a spatial beyond that is no less sinister in its purposes than the temporal abyss.

Such figures are phantom-like; but like statues they make their appearance in a daytime context from which they derive a particular strangeness: it is as if the substitution of a daylight setting for the nocturnal haunting of traditional ghosts gave their ghostliness an unexpectedly "everyday" character of its own. The swan's strangeness, it is true, derives only from the fact that it is out-of-place in the dusty street, far from its "beau lac natal" ("Le Cygne," line 22). In other respects it is an ordinary bird. Just like the *petites vieilles,* the eponymous *passante,* and the *sept vieillards* are figures that it is not in itself surprising to meet in the streets; they are "at home" there. It is rather a certain spectral character—as apparitions, a ghostly form of dimensionality—that confers on such homely figures their uncanny character, while exerting the further effect of making the street itself strange in turn. As daylight specters, "spectres en plein jour," they are something like everyday ghosts, familiar phantoms, whose function is to reveal the street itself, their abode, as itself unexpectedly *connected,* allied in like fashion with an otherwise unexpected dimension of alterity, and serving, therefore, as a channel of communication, not solely with other streets, but also with another dimension of the world.

In developing such an atmosphere of everyday uncanniness in poems like "Les sept vieillards" (poem 90) and "À une passante" (poem 93), Baudelaire took a hint from Gautier, who in "Vieux de la vieille" (*Emaux et Camées*), had imagined the city's theater district—"le long du boulevard"—as the site of a Napoleonic visitation on the occasion of exercises that heralded the *coup d'état* of December 2, 1851—the event that was to make Louis-Napoléon emperor:

Par l'ennui chassé de ma chambre,
J'errais le long du boulevard;
Il faisait un temps de décembre,
Vent froid, fine pluie et brouillard.

Et là je vis, spectacle étrange,
Echappés du sombre séjour,
Sous la bruine et dans la fange,
Passer des spectres en plein jour.
. . . .

Mais des spectres près du Gymnase,
A deux pas des Variétés,
Sans brume ou linceul qui les gaze,
Des spectres mouillés et crottés!
etc.[1]

(Driven by boredom from my room,
I wandered along the boulevard;
it was December weather,
with a cold wind, light rain, and fog.

And there I saw, a strange spectacle,
escaping from the domain of darkness
and passing by in the mist and slush,
a group of daylight specters.
....
But specters near the Gymnase,
a step or two from the Variétés,
without fog or winding sheet to soften their outlines,
Specters wet and muddy!
etc.)

It is very unlikely to have been the poem's frankly Bonapartist politics that attracted Baudelaire's favorable attention. But specters devoid of shrouds, ghosts in wet clothing and with mud on their boots! Daytime specters, haunting the familiar city streets on an unsurprisingly foggy December day: "Vent froid, fine pluie et brouillard!" Specters of undecidable status, then, as apparently real as they are self-evidently ghostly! Here was something new. It is this *indeterminacy* of the everyday and the ghostly that makes this poem, down to its matter-of-fact octosyllables, indelibly memorable: "la chose vaut qu'on la regarde," as the text itself puts it, something worth looking at.

Gautier draws out the ambiguity over several stanzas. But finally—and disappointingly—he makes it quite clear that his specters are not at all the ghosts of long-dead *grognards* (grunts) of the Imperial Army, returning to life in celebration of the return of Empire. They are merely a group of elderly veterans—"quelques vieux de la vieille / Qui célébraient le grand retour" (a few old veterans celebrating the grand return)—faintly if endearingly ridiculous and indisputably real in their now ill-fitting uniforms. Baudelaire, in contrast, taking up Gautier's hint, will grasp the value of a practice of permanent (or at least extended) undecidability as something more than just a witty trick, and will make it the crucial feature of an allegorical poetics that defines the city as a space of contact and mutual crossing-over. The street in particular becomes a site of encounter that straddles the spheres of everyday reality and an otherwise unknowable transcendence—spheres that are assumed to exist in chiasmically "rhyming" relation with each other, and thus to engage in a permanent exchange of properties that recalls the fetish aesthetics, albeit in a now more sinister mode, of earlier times. And Gautier's "daylight specter" will become, for Baudelaire, the crucial atmospheric figure, the everyday apparition that indexes the existence of such a chiasmic space of uncanny mediation.

The opening lines of "Les sept vieillards" allude quite specifically to Gautier, then. But they do so within the wholly Baudelairean context of a noisy chiasmus centering on the word *cité* and situating "le spectre en plein jour" as the city's indexical epiphenomenon.

> Fourmillante cité, cité pleine de rêves,
> Où le spectre en plein jour raccroche le passant!

The city, as *civitas*—a social entity—is here mapped as being, interchangeably, *composed of crowds* ("fourmillante") and *crowded with dreams* ("pleine de rêves"). Although it is divided, its two *composantes* (crowds and dreams) are inseparable and arise each as an aspect of the other, the "spectre en plein jour" being the very figure of their inseparability, given that it is described, by the verb *raccrocher,* as simultaneously and interchangeably an everyday beggar or prostitute plucking at the sleeve of the passerby, and a dream phenomenon experienced in waking life: Capturing the engaged attention of the self-same innocent *passant* by virtue of its oneiric strangeness, the daylight specter marks the center point of the chiasmic city, the intersection of the spatial *X* where encounter occurs; and it does so by virtue of the metaphoric versatility of a verb that has meanings both trivial and abstract, simultaneously vulgar and intellectual (cf. *hook* in English). Nevertheless—and this is the implication of the chiasmus, its figural significance—the same interchangeability of opposed properties that the daylight specter makes manifest also characterizes the full extent of each side of the chiasmus. I mean that the "cité pleine de rêves" is identical with, and shares the same space as, the city of busy streets and frenetic human activity; while the city-as-crowded-ant-bed is permeated, less obviously perhaps but no less certainly, with the stuff of dreams. The two do not alternate, for example, according to day- or nighttime, but interpenetrate.

We might say, then, that the area of chiasmus presents a map of the city's *atmosphere,* understanding that word to name the epiphenomenal effect exerted by the whole city—the *ville* or *urbs*—when, crowded with people as with dreams, the city is understood as the site of a social configuration, a *civitas.* And if so, we might add that *atmosphere* arises, therefore, as an effect of the city's noisy *inhabitedness,* where inhabitedness implies also hauntedness; it is synonymous, in other words, with the urban crowd and the electricity it generates as it surges through the streets, its collective moods determining something like the variable weather—*le temps qu'il fait* in its relation to *le temps qui passe*—of community. And surely the true subject of "Les sept vieillards" is none other, therefore, than urban crowdedness and its (everyday) spectrality or power to haunt. That would be why, of all Baudelaire's treatments of the urban thematic, this is the poem whose writing is most incontrovertibly a writing of atmosphere, but of atmosphere understood as something crowded and multiplicitous like foggy weather: *le temps qu'il fait dans la cité* or city weather.

"Les sept vieillards"

The mutual interference of the oneiric in the everyday, like that of the ordinary in the uncanny, produces in the city a permanent expenditure of *energy*: a reverberation of noise like that so amply signaled, in line 12:[2] "Le faubourg secoué par les lourds tombereaux," by the line's rhythmic regularity (3–3/3–3), its repeated vowel ("faubourg," "secoué," "lourd"), its association of *b* and *r* (in "faubourg" and "tombereaux") in a way reminiscent of the words "brume" (line 6) and "brouillard" (line 9), and finally, of course, by the presence of the word "tombe" in the "tombereaux" that are themselves reminiscent of the revolutionary Terror. In this respect, the line functions as a first fulfillment of the implications of the opening chiasmus: "Fourmillante cité, cité pleine de rêves," which furnishes in its opening syllable, and the *mouillement* of its first word, much of the phonetic and even thematic material of the lines that follow. What intervenes, however, in the poem's three opening quatrains, is on the one hand the vision of a city become waterlogged to the point of extremity—its air space invaded by "brume" and "brouillard," its streets become "canaux étroits" brimming with mystery, the houses simulating "les deux quais d'une rivière accrue"—and on the other the narrative corresponding to this "décor semblable à l'âme de l'acteur," the account of the poet-speaker's soul, similarly penetrated by debilitating noise in the form of an invasive lassitude, a loss of moral energy. The city's atmosphere, clogged with watery particles as it is crowded with people and dreams, itself exerts a deleterious effect on the morale of one who—in this respect not unlike the poet of "Le soleil," fencing his way "le long du vieux faubourg"—seeks to resist the power of its entropic liquefaction, and to refuse or ignore the significance of its anonymous, fragmented and fragmenting multiplicity, the meaning of its threatening omnipresence as the weather of the "fourmillante cité."

When the first of the spectral old men suddenly pops up, then (lines 13–17: "Tout à coup, un vieillard . . . / M'apparut"), his apparition signifies the final disintegration of the subject's remaining will to resist the all-penetrating atmosphere, that is, the moment of his disalienation, when a certain cosmic state of affairs can no longer be ignored or denied. This "spectre en plein jour" appears, then, as a kind of condensation of the ambient atmosphere or an emanation from out of its damp fogginess, as is suggested by the match of the color of his rags with that of the "ciel pluvieux," and by the prevalence—in the description of his appearance (which "aurait *fait pleuvoir* les aumônes" were it not for the evil gleam in his eye, with its "prunelle *trempée* dans le fiel")—of a lexicon of dampness and saturation (lines 14–16). The angularity of his physique, meanwhile—it makes him look "cassé, son échine / Faisant avec sa jambe un parfait angle droit," while his stick gives him the appearance, and the clumsy gait, "D'un quadripède infirme ou d'un juif à trois pattes"—endows him with a distinct family resemblance to the dislocated anatomy of the *petites vieilles,* with their also angular shape (and their evil puppet master). And finally, like Gautier's ancient guardsmen, he is, as an apparition, disconcertingly real in a quite physical sense, as he determinedly battles with the wintry slush of the street in a kind of externalization of his hostility to the universe: "Dans la neige et la boue il allait s'empêtrant, / Comme s'il écrasait des morts sous ses savates" (lines 26–27). Simultaneously personifying the mystery flowing like sludge in the "canaux étroits" that are the city's streets, and the thick fog of its all-penetrating wintry ambience, he is marked also as an ambassador of the principle of Evil whose manifestation is Time.

Above all, however, he contains in himself a principle of multiplication that stamps him, together with the replicas of himself that now (lines 29–36) begin to proliferate, as constituting also a figure of the crowd and of its infinite and anonymous *fourmillement.* Gautier's "spectres en plein jour" were already a cohesive group of "vieux de la vieille," but differentiated both by their uniforms ("Trois fantômes de vieux grognards, / En uniforme de l'ex-garde, / Avec deux ombres de hussards") and by their contrasting degrees of corpulence ("L'un a maigri, l'autre grossi"). By contrast, Baudelaire's "spectre en plein jour" (in the singular) becomes a plural—"ces spectres baroques" (line 31)—but only under the specific condition of an absolute identity, that of a single "sinistre vieillard qui se multipliait" (line 32). The initial split into two ("Son pareil le suivait: barbe, oeil, dos, bâton, loques, / Nul trait ne distinguait, du même enfer venu, / Ce jumeau centenaire") simply reproduces itself at regular intervals ("de minute en minute," line 35), until the rhythm of this multiplication of identical old men seems likely, "malgré tant de décrépitude," to go on forever.

So to investigate whence arises the sensation of the uncanny that they convey is to identify a number of sources. In part it arises from the strange determination they display, the obstinacy with which they advance, in lockstep, "vers un but inconnu." But it comes too from the unexpected reconciliation of the one and the many, that is, the "fourmillement" that makes them a figure of the unparticularized, anonymous urban crowd. Finally and perhaps primarily, this self-multiplying figure is uncanny because of the impossible amalgam it simultaneously presents of the time-bound—the tatters and ugliness, the "décrépitude" that makes them monstrous—with the eternal:

> Que celui-là qui rit de mon inquiétude,
> Et qui n'est pas saisi d'un frisson fraternel,
> Songe bien que malgré tant de décrépitude
> Ces sept monstres avaient l'air éternel!
>
> (lines 37–40)

For such features as these are those of Baudelairean allegory, understood as a perception that the everyday real is capable at any moment of revealing an atmospheric stratum whose function—like that of the messenger from the beyond that is a daytime specter, be it a statue, a writhing swan, a misshapen or dislocated human or other fetish-like figure—is to convey an intimation of lived time as a manifestation of supernaturalist evil. And simultaneously they describe the crowded city as itself the crucial locus of the allegorical mode of disalienation through supernaturalist insight: the "cité pleine de rêves" that is "fourmillante" because it is the habitat of the crowd. The sinister old men of the poem are thus, simultaneously, *allegorical figures,* exerting their effect of disalienation on the now captivated, no longer heroically resistant, subject of the poem, and *figures of the urban crowd* as itself a site of allegory, by virtue of its combined qualities of oneness and multiplicity, of real presence in the here and now and allusion to eternity. It is in this latter capacity that they manifest the atmosphere of urban weather as *le temps qu'il fait*: while in the former their multiplication functions as a manifestation of *le temps qui passe*, as these two lines make particularly clear:

> Car je comptai sept fois, *de minute en minute*,
> Ce sinistre vieillard qui se multipliait!
>
> (lines 35–36; my emphasis)

Allegory, then, to sum up, is a name for the atmosphere of the city, which it identifies as the foggy weather generated by the city's ant bed multiplicity, its surging crowd. Urban weather in turn manifests the mystery of time, as the minute-by-minute process of multiplication, beyond which can be glimpsed the sinister force of eternity. It follows that the gales and hurricanes of history—subliminally present in "Les sept vieillards" in the word "tombereaux" of line 12 as well as in the poem's reminiscence of Gautier's "Vieux de la vieille"—are likewise meteorological manifestations of time, but in the form of violent and destructive events that cannot be ignored. They are indicators of the same transcendent force of evil—the same "eternity"—that the daily weather of passing time alludes to more subtly, as the eventual product of its minute-by-minute multiplication. Allegory, in short, makes apparent—indeed apparitional—in the form of an atmospherics of everyday city life, the noise of time that is *le temps qu'il fait* in relation to *le temps qui passe*.

The remainder of the poem is devoted, however, to the consequences for human subjects of the kind of abruptly expanded consciousness—the glimpse of horror—that results from allegorical encounter. Whereas "Le Cygne" identifies melancholia as a long-term psychic outcome of disalienation, and "À une passante" (as we shall see) explores in its tercets the epistemological dilemma—both the wondering and the wonderment—that is entailed by knowing only that one doesn't know, "Les sept vieillards" offers a vivid account of the immediate moral panic that besets one who is "blessé par le mystère et l'absurdité" (line 48). A glimpse of eternity has the impact of a wound, a brush with death. It reveals time as a force both inexorable and ironic, inscrutable in its almost mechanical quality of self-reproduction, of endless birth and rebirth:

> Aurais-je sans mourir contemplé le huitième,
> Sosie inexorable, ironique et fatal,
> Dégoûtant Phénix, fils et père de lui-même?
>
> (lines 41–43)

The alien character of such a force—its mystery and absurdity in the eyes of time-bound creatures—provokes denial:

> —Mais je tournai le dos au cortège infernal.
>
> ....
>
> Je rentrai, je fermai la porte, épouvanté
>
> (lines 44 and 46)

But denial being itself a mode of acknowledgement of that which it seeks to deny, the mystery and absurdity provoke also an exasperated sense of disequilibrium, the mental drunkenness whose salient symptom is the sensation of allegorical vision as seeing double (line 45). So it is as if the apparently infinite doubling of the old man produces in turn the double vision of split subjectivity. One sees *something,* but something one cannot grasp, something that one knows is impossible to "see," not solely in the sense that it is beyond vision but also because, as the infinite, it is beyond human understanding, beyond our "ken."[3]

It is this destabilizing sense of doubleness, then—a sense akin to the Hegelian dilemma of the *bekannt* that cannot therefore be *erkannt,* and one of course already inherent in the poem's opening chiasmus—that returns now. But it returns both magnified and intensified, as a consequence of the intervening encounter with the multiplying "spectre en plein jour" that has *brought it home,* as it were, to the subjective consciousness of the poem's speaker. It is as if the world of the "cité," modeled already in lines 1–2 as a noisy chiasmus, has transferred its disequilibrium and loss of control to a pre-Rimbaldian "bateau ivre," a drunken boat that is metaphoric not of the city, but of a "reason" and a "soul"—an individual—helplessly tempest-tossed on the monstrously shoreless sea of the infinite.

> Vainement ma raison voulait prendre la barre,
> La tempête en jouant déroutait ses efforts,
> Et mon âme dansait, dansait, vieille gabarre
> Sans mâts, sur une mer monstrueuse et sans bords!
>
> (lines 49–52)

This new, crazily unbalanced chiasmus of the final lines is dependent, like the initial figure, on the noisy semantics of apposition ("mon âme" / "vieille gabarre" compares in this respect with "fourmillante" / "pleine de rêves"). But in addition it is "monstrously" extended, now, by a *rejet* that upsets the rhythmic balance, not only of the chiasmus itself, but also of the regularly aligned metrical units that are these still classical verses. Thus is made sensible to the reader, by poetic means, the destabilizing impact of a disruption of supposedly normal order that has become at once cosmic in its scope—no longer confined to the limits of a city—and in its effect monstrous, by virtue of the disalienating revelation of the alien character of the world.

This intensification of an initial noise to the point of monstrosity—*noise,* by the way, derives from *nausea,* the sensation that accompanies loss of balance, *noisy* and *noisome* being cognates—results from the event of encounter that is the apparition, at the poem's midpoint, of the "sept monstres hideux" with their "air éternel." So it is as if the foggy weather, the moisture-laden atmosphere of the beginning, reaches a point of saturation where it condenses into the spectral apparition of the hideous figure(s) of time, and in so doing becomes, for the poem's protagonist, both the vehicle and the occasion of an event of consciousness experienced as the onset of a tempest—the tempest, that is, of history. The power of the everyday specter as a phenomenon of city atmospherics is, then, to demonstrate the solidarity of the *passing time* of daily life, figured by the minute-by-minute multiplication of identical old men, with the devastating and disruptive *occurrences* that are recognized as events of history, the latter emerging without discontinuity from the former, by virtue of a phenomenon comparable with the way a storm evolves out of the build-up of atmospheric pressure that precedes and produces it, as if it were a precipitate of that heavy and foreboding atmosphere.

If historical events, in "Le Cygne" for example, produce in those who undergo them the form of consciousness I am calling disalienation (whose long-term effect is melancholy), then to become disalienated, as the speaker protagonist of "Les sept vieillards" does, is in turn to experience an *event*: an event of one's personal history such as that recorded in the poem, and one whose short-term effect is the destabilization induced by double vision. As line 45 puts it, one is worn down, "exaspéré comme un ivrogne qui voit double," where exasperation refers, by etymology, to an experience of asperity or roughness—one that is both an aggravation of intensity and an intensification of aggravation, wearing away the already weakened resistance of one's "âme déjà lasse" (line 11). So the condition of such disalienation is one's "exasperating" long-term exposure, by virtue of participation in the daily life of the "fourmillante cité" that is simultaneously "pleine de rêves," to the weather of time that is the atmospherics of the urban crowd.

Time that passes, the time of the everyday, becomes historical time, then, the time of events (including the event of disalienation) as a consequence of the build-up of entropy, or exasperation, that might be referred to as weathering. And as its title indicates, "À une passante" is the poem in which Baudelaire pursues his exploration of the (therefore allegorical) relation of passing time to the violently disalienating weather of the crowded street that constitutes history's eventfulness. The encounter of which the famous sonnet speaks constitutes the disalienating *event* of a *passing by*: one in which, furthermore, the mediating factor is once more the atmosphere of the crowd.

"À une passante"

À une passante

La rue assourdissante autour de moi hurlait.
Longue, mince, en grand deuil, douleur majestueuse,
Une femme passa, d'une main fastueuse
Soulevant, balançant le feston et l'ourlet;

Agile et noble, avec sa jambe de statue.
Moi, je buvais, crispé comme un extravagant,
Dans son œil, ciel livide où germe l'ouragan,
La douceur qui fascine et le plaisir qui tue.

Un éclair . . . puis la nuit!—Fugitive beauté
Dont le regard m'a fait soudainement renaître,
Ne te verrai-je plus que dans l'éternité?

Ailleurs, bien loin d'ici! trop tard! jamais peut-être!
Car j'ignore où tu fuis, tu ne sais où je vais,
Ô toi que j'eusse aimée, ô toi qui le savais!

In Passing

The traffic roared around me, deafening!
Tall, slender, in mourning—noble grief—
a woman passed, and with a jewelled hand
gathered up her black embroidered hem;

stately yet lithe, as if a statue walked. . .
And trembling like a fool, I drank from eyes
as ashen as the clouds before a gale
the grace that beckons and the joy that kills.

Lightning . . . then darkness! Lovely fugitive
whose glance has brought me back to life! But where
is life—not this side of eternity?

Elsewhere! Too far, too late, or never at all!
Of me you know nothing, I nothing of you—you
whom I might have loved and who knew that too!

There are biographical reasons why hideous old men and an elegantly dressed widow in full mourning might appear in Baudelaire as interchangeable figures in the role of daylight specter. The poet's model of the devastating intervention of history in human lives, as we've seen, is the tempest or hurricane, which figures here at line 7. But his model for the emotional effect of disalienation as the outcome of history's ravages is rooted, it seems, in the remarriage of his mother to the despised and hated figure of General Aupick, following the death of Baudelaire's father—the event that is generally understood to frame, in particular, the nostalgic tone of a poem such as "Je n'ai pas oublié . . . ." So if the evil old men, as figures of passing time, refer to a hellish infinite of eternity from which the protagonist and speaking subject of "Les sept vieillards" shrinks and turns away in shock, the ambiguously (but detectably) whorish widow of "À une passante" is, for all her fashionable elegance, no less a "spectre en plein jour" passing, like time itself, in the deafeningly noise-ridden street, and thus, as we'll see, a figure of *modern*—that is disalienating—beauty, as opposed to beauty *tout court.*

In the terms of "Le peintre de la vie moderne," she is, then, "l'élément relatif, circonstantiel" (the relative, circumstantial element) that refers to, but cannot reproduce, an absolute of beauty, itself an "élément éternel, invariable" (an eternal, invariable element), and one beyond direct apprehension, since it can be manifested only in contingent form. And her coquetry makes her simultaneously an updated version of Andromache, regretful of lost dignity but a tarnished survivor, and inclined to opportunism in the circumstances of the present: "Veuve d'Hector, hélas! et femme d'Hélénus!" The widow's "douleur majesteuse" is thus not at all incompatible with the enticing display, whether inadvertent or intentional, of her "jambe de statue" and the "main fastueuse" that so elegantly sets her garments asway: "Soulevant, balançant le feston et l'ourlet." In short, with her flirtatious charm, she is adept at the skill prescribed in "Les sept vieillards" (line 2) for daylight specters and described in the words "raccroche[r] le passant."

But the key difference between the two structurally equivalent allegorical poems with their opposed but concordant figures of the absolute lies therefore in the apparently opposed responses of the narrative *I* in each poem. The speaking subject of the sonnet is motivated by the "passante's" fascinating beauty *not* to turn away, and not to shut himself in his room like the badly shaken subject of "Les sept vieillards." Instead, he succumbs willingly to the desire she inspires, giving himself over to it fully as his eyes drink in the powerful and dangerous draught proffered by her own fascinating, albeit deadly, glance:

> Moi je buvais, crispé comme un extravagant,

> Dans son œil, ciel livide où germe l'ouragan,
> La douceur qui fascine et le plaisir qui tue.
>
> (lines 6–8)

The word *tue*—not coincidentally rhyming at the end of the quatrains with the word *rue* at their outset—comes as a shock, then, to the reader just as it does to the narrator of the poem. It is as if the nascent hurricane glimpsed in the pale sky of the *passante*'s eye had suddenly struck, demonstrating its identity with so many other storms and tempests in Baudelaire, including the one that tosses the "vieille gabarre" of the speaker's soul in "Les sept vieillards." The encounter with the beautiful and statuesque widow is no less an encounter with death and with history, no less a moment of devastating disalienation, than is the apparition of the uncannily multiplying old men.

As for the demoralizing loss of confidence and control that results in "À une passante," as in "Les sept vieillards," from the allegorical effect of "seeing double," this is once again a consequence of disalienation. If we take the meeting of glances that occurs at the heart of "À une passante" as a symbolic equivalent of the sexual act itself, then an astonishing *fusée* dating, like the sonnet from the early 1860s, is relevant. In it, "l'acte d'amour" (the act of love) is described as sharing with torture and surgery (as surgery was practiced before the discovery of anesthetics, of course) not excruciating pain *per se*, but what I take to be for Baudelaire its moral and psychological equivalent: the dispossession of one's selfhood, the depersonalization that one of the two participants in such alarming encounters necessarily undergoes. This is what Baudelaire calls "une sorte de décomposition" (a kind of coming apart); and he describes it in a striking comment: "—Épouvantable jeu où il faut que l'un des joueurs perde le gouvernement de soi-même!" (*OC* 1:651, cf. also 659; a horrifying game in which one of the players has to lose control over his- or herself). One thinks of the "Muselmänner" described by Primo Levi and other Holocaust witnesses as reduced to "bare life," a kind of living death.[4] And such a bereft state of absurd living-on is the outcome of the disalienating encounter that the protagonist of "Les sept vieillards" describes in terms of loss of control: "Vainement ma raison voulait prendre la barre," and so on (where the word *gouvernail* suggests itself as a synonym for this now useless rudder bar). But the same absurd and bereft outcome is implied also by the self-description of the speaker of "À une passante," who at the moment of eye contact is "crispé comme un extravagant," the etymological implication of the word *extravagant* being that his mind—the seat of controlling reason—has gone wandering.

The pain that the act of love shares with surgery and torture—the *fusée* speaks, for example, of muscles contracted "comme sous l'action d'une pile galvanique" (as if jolted by a galvanic battery)—is not so much physical pain, then, as it is a moral suffering: the awareness of lost self-governance that is a consequence of disalienation. And the encounter with a daylight specter in the street, be it in the form of hideously self-replicating old men or of a single beautiful *passante,* shares with torture, surgery, and the act of love that same sense of painful amputation from one's former self. For it is not just a matter of lost self-governance; the pain arises also from the evidence that one's supposed self-governance has therefore always been something of an illusion. Given the power now understood to be exerted by the previously unrecognized Enemy that is time, disalienation does not solely strip us of our self-mastery and control. By revealing the extent of our helpless subservience to time and to a history we can neither govern nor predict, it shows that we have *never* been in real control of our lives. The gain in lucidity is undeniable. But it serves only to confirm our state of helplessness vis-à-vis the evil principle of eternity that governs our life, the puppet master of "Les petites vieilles."

And so, in "À une passante," the confident declarative sentences of the quatrains give way in the tercets to anxious and anguished questioning, to pained exclamations, and to an acknowledgment both of what *can* be known, and of the severe limits placed on human knowledge. These reflections represent the moral and mental equivalent of the drunken imbalance experienced by the devastated speaker of "Les sept vieillards" and expressed by him as the exasperation of double vision:

> Car j'ignore où tu fuis, tu ne sais où je vais,
> O toi que j'eusse aimée, ô toi qui le savais!
>
> (lines 13–14)

Here it is, the figure of apostrophe that captures the new (dis) orientation of the speaker's attention and concern. Restricted in the quatrains to a flâneur's interest in the here and now of the street and the crowd from which the *passante* appears to emerge, his attention and address are now "turned away" (apostrephein), and directed toward another dimension of things altogether—the sphere toward which the "fugitive beauté" (line 9), to whose glance he owes what he calls his rebirth, is fleeing, or indeed has taken flight. This is a sphere at once acknowledged in its reality and recognized as beyond the reach of the positive knowledge that informs the quatrains, concerned as they are with the familiar urban scene. Beset from the start by anticipatory noise, "la rue assourdissante," the former flâneur, idly observing the immediate scene, is now a figure of disalienation. Newly conscious of eternity ("Ne te verrai-je plus que dans l'éternité?"), he is deeply disturbed, and indeed devastated, by his nascent awareness of the split cosmos into which he has gained some, at best partial, insight; and concerned, as well, by the implications of that split, of which he remains uncertain and questioning.

That this newly perceived universe is structured chiasmically is suggested, of course, by the pattern of approach and flight, convergence and divergence, that defines the relation of the *passante* to the stationary flâneur, as well as by the intersection of their glances at the sonnet's turn. But the fact that the male subject of the encounter is stationary while it is the *passante* who approaches and then moves on has the effect of distorting the perceived chiasmic structure, and of making its perception noisy. Rather than an *X*, one is led to imagine a *V*-like pattern of encounter; or indeed a simple transverse line traced tangentially to the observer by the moving *passante* as she passes by. Furthermore, in "Les sept vieillards," we saw an already noisy chiasmus become considerably more disturbed and unsteady in response to a disalienating encounter with a daylight specter; and something similar is visible in "À une passante." For here it is not solely that the narrative chiasmus that maps onto the overall structure of the sonnet, with its intersection at the poem's turn, has become distorted. It is also that a chiasmic patterning discernible, as in "Les sept vieillards," at the opening and the conclusion of the poem is also so noisy here as to be barely recognizable as such. Assailed as he is by street noise at the start and barely able, at the end, to do more than gesture in the direction of a chiasmic vision of the universe, what the poem makes readable in its subject is thus a history of the noise-ridden consciousness of the world that is his. And, as in "Les sept vieillards," that history concerns the loss of "gouvernement de soi," the "espèce de décomposition" that is the consequence of a disalienating encounter.

The opening line—"La rue assourdissante autour de moi hurlait"—forms an already severely distorted chiasmus, one that seems positively invaded by the street racket of which it speaks, to the point where, unlike the opening chiasmus of "Les sept vieillards," it is scarcely recognizable as such. Only the rhythmic pattern (2-4-4-2) conforms to a strictly chiasmic structure here; the phonetic inversion of "La rue" in "hurlait" ([lary]/(yrlɛ]) is approximate and at best suggestive, while "assourdissante" and "autour de moi" present a slight phonetic echo anchored by the vowel [u] of "ass*ourd*issante" and "aut*our de*" together with a degree of semantic redundancy (street noise is deafening in that it surrounds the hearer, and invasive to the extent that it is deafening). The consciousness of the *I*, his sense of selfhood, is already under severe attack, then. But in the tercets—although the elements of a possible chiasmus are clearly present in the parallelism of the final two lines—the figure itself remains unrealized and appears only as an obscurely glimpsed but unactualized virtuality of chiasmus, the parallel construction reflecting disconnected rather than "rhyming" worlds. With the flight of the *passante,* the narrative subject's ability to grasp the pattern of the universe has been shattered; he can now only shuffle the components of its allegorical structure. And to understand the nature of the chiasmic encounter that has brought about such a disintegration of the subject and his world—the latter falling apart, as it seems, in response to the "decomposition" of the former—we must return to the midpoint of the sonnet: the place where it turns, the hinge point of its own dual structure.

For the positional equivalence of the first line of the quatrains and the first hemistich of the tercets invites their comparison. Line 1 sets the stage for the narrative to come of the *passante*'s approach, and the first hemistich of line 9 has a similar stage-setting function. As a retrospective account of the narrative *I*'s experience of the annihilating hurricane he has glimpsed in the eye of the *passante*—the event that, between its "germination" in line 8 and its retrospective recapitulation in line 9, has therefore occurred in the blank space of the turn itself (the sonnet's own eye)—the recapitulative hemistich ("Un éclair . . . puis la nuit!") accounts for, and situates, the anxious series of reflections and speculations, the questions and anguished ejaculations that follow. But where the speaker of the poem positions himself at the center of the street scene in line 1, as if he were the target of the deafening noise that surrounds him, the midpoint of the hemistich of line 9 (between the notations of a lightning flash and of the ensuing darkness) is occupied by . . . an ellipsis—a sign of elision. More particularly, the deafened *I* of line I, situated as central by the phrase "autour de moi," occupies by implication the place of that line's (central) caesura, while the equivalent of that central position in the first hemistich of line 9 is the site of the ellipsis. So what is enacted between lines 1 and 9, it seems, is a history of the *néantisation* or annulment of the poem's central consciousness—a history in two stages, of which the second amounts to the momentary suppression of that consciousness if not its actual disappearance. Notice that "assourdissant" suggests the idea of muting, a diminishment of strength, as well as indicating deafness proper. It is, then, as if the central consciousness of the poem, established from the start as a presence already attacked by noise, has undergone an actual deletion in the space of the sonnet's turn, where his eyes meet the glance of the *passante*. Between the moment of the lightning flash and his awareness of darkness, suggesting a return to consciousness—the moment that records his experience of the event as it is retrospectively resumed at line 9—he has been *absent from himself*.

In other words, his looking into the eyes of the *passante* ("où germe l'ouragan") has been the occasion of his losing his self-presence, "le gouvernement de soi-même," to a power infinitely greater then he, a force whose power of "assourdissement," manifested as noise, has concentrated into the hurricane in the eye of the *passante*—that is, of one who, personifying the passage of time, herself passes by. A hurricane is a storm that turns—a little as a sonnet turns, perhaps, but violently and destructively—around its own inactive center, its so-called eye. It enacts in this way the concept of entropy, etymologically a turning inward, along with entropy's power to bring about what Baudelaire calls a falling apart: "une espèce de décomposition." In the eye of the *passante,* who figures time, the deadly entropic storm circles around another eye, one that is a center of nothingness.

If chiasmus is the figure that describes the allegorical structure of the cosmos in a spatial perspective, there is also a power of temporality, then, one that is active within that structure, taking as it does the form of ultimately destructive noise, to the point of "decomposing" it. To glimpse that power, whose destructive passing-by is experienced as history, is to experience one's own "espèce de décomposition" as a loss of self-governance, and in doing so to suffer disalienation, the lightning flash of illumination whose cost is that one learns the extent of one's vulnerability and ignorance. All Baudelaire's survivor figures—be they the *petites vieilles* one meets in the street; Andromache or her allegorical other, the swan; the narrator of "Les sept vieillards," or the one of "À une passante," with his experience of encounter—are figures who, having looked into the eye of the hurricane, absurdly live on in this way, as witness to the existence of the evil controlling power, engaged in the horrifying game, the "épouvantable jeu," called history, that governs the world. Traumatized testimonial figures, they survive their encounter with time among the ruins of their own destroyed "gouvernement de soi-même," the narrators among them no less allegorical in their function, finally, than the daylight specters whose encounter they relate.

The model in rhetoric for time's destructive passing by, what humans know as history, is given to us in "À une passante" as the particular mode of elision that is called preterition. From the Latin *praeter-ire* (to move forward), preterition names the practice of mentioning, in passing, that which, relevant as it may be, will not be the object of further discursive attention. Preterition marginalizes or passes over, in this way, what it thus characterizes as expendable, setting it aside as the discourse moves on to other matters. And as a consequence the object of preterition enters the category of the preterite, of that which, like the *I* figure of "À une passante," and like Baudelaire's other survivor figures, is left behind or left over, bereft and abandoned. The French *preterite,* also known as the *passé simple,* contrasts with the imperfect, or continuous past, as the verb tense reserved for that which has undergone the fate of preterition and become residual—one of history's victims, surviving into a present to which it is no longer relevant. What is at stake in "À une passante," then, and what similarly haunts the *fusée* in which the act of love is compared to torture and surgery, is therefore *the pain of becoming such a preterite object*: the loser in the "épouvantable jeu" of history who, undergoing "une espèce de décomposition," survives the loss of selfhood as a figure of bare life—the leftover of his or her own former, not-yet-disalienated self. The only remaining function such a figure can exercise is that of bearing witness, whether passively (like the swan, Andromache, or the *petites vieilles*), or actively, as Baudelaire's narrator figures do, telling their story of encounter and of its preteritive effects as an *exemplum* or allegory, and thus as an act of testimony.

Of the three instances of preterition in "À une passante," I have already noted the elision, in the first hemistich of line 9, of the narrator's presence to his own consciousness, an elision that recapitulates the crucial meeting of glances—"the act of love"—that was itself announced, but elided, at the sonnet's turn. It is significant that in French the sign of an ellipsis (. . .) is called *points de suspension*. The effect of the elision in line 9 is that the narrator figure is indeed left hanging, as it were: suspended for all eternity, as the *passante* moves on and away, into the unknown. A second instance of preterition, then, is in the sonnet's title, which—somewhat as in Goethe's title, "An die ferne Geliebte" (To the Distant Beloved)—enacts the paradox of addressing one who is simultaneously described as in the process of becoming absent: moving away, passing out of range, beyond earshot. Preterition as passing by here makes address a form of apostrophe. So the enunciatory subject of the titular apostrophe is self-described as always already suspended, caught in the process of being left behind; and it becomes the role of the remaining history of preterition to confirm his abandonment. Positionally equivalent as it is to the imperfect tense of the stage-setting "hurlait" at the end of line 1, the contrasting preterite of the verb *passer* at the end of the first hemistich of line 2 ("une femme passa") does so by making explicit what, as a virtuality, was already implicit in the title. For to speak in the preterite tense of the action of passing is to acknowledge both the "passedness" and the pastness to which the subject of speech is henceforth relegated. It is just that, as we have seen, to be passed in this way is to remain suspended: the object of a preterition survives his own demise, as it were, living on in abandonment.

So, if the elision at the center of the first hemistich of line 9 refers to the speaking subject's loss of consciousness/self-governance, we are now in a position to supply—from the title, and more specifically from line 3—the missing third-person preterite verb that corresponds to his subjective loss. The objective correlative of *his* loss is *her* passing by, passing *him* by. Consequently, the elision that I read earlier as "un éclair [je perdis conscience] puis la nuit!" (a lightning flash [I lost consciousness] then night) might equally be expressed as "Un éclair [elle passa] puis la nuit!" (A lightning flash [she passed by] then darkness!). And the mutual substitutability of "elle passa" and "je perdis conscience/le gouvernement de moi-même" corresponds, of course, to the significance of the buried metaphor (too trite, perhaps, to be made explicit?) that governs the whole poem. I mean that of the "coup de foudre" as simultaneously a lightning strike and love at first sight, at once a meteorological-metaphysical disaster and the birth of erotic desire, as in "l'acte d'amour" described in the *fusée*. The metaphor figures disalienation, understood as the death of a certain self subject to illusion—the illusion of "gouvernement de soi-même"—and the congruent emergence of a self newly aware, albeit aware only of deprivation and desire in a world, governed by time, that is alien: alien to our own wishes, alien to our knowledge and to our governance. A world become absurd, then; one that escapes our grasp and "passes" our understanding. *Un monde qui nous dépasse . . .*

This "coup de foudre" effect of disalienation—a certain form of death accompanied by a certain experience of rebirth ("Fugitive beauté / Dont le regard m'a fait soudain renaître") would be, in particular, the property of what Baudelaire elsewhere calls modern beauty: a beauty whose "composition double" makes it a phenomenon at once *contingent*—simultaneously fugitive and mnemonic, by virtue of its alliance with time and history—and *absolute*: able, that is, to convey a glimpse of the transcendence, supernatural and awe-inspiring, that lies behind and beyond that screen of temporality and leaves one thunderstruck. Modern beauty as a preteritional phenomenon, then, is one that simultaneously seduces the observer and strikes at his/her sense of self, abandoning the disalienated viewer, as it moves on toward new forms of historicity, to a permanent sense of deprivation and dissatisfaction, divided between nostalgia for an irretrievable past and curiosity concerning an unknowable future: "ne te verrai-je plus que dans l'éternité?"[5]

What such an art of atmosphere and the "coup de foudre," changeable like the weather, cannot vouchsafe, however, is permanence and stability. It makes impossible the security of a relation—be it to an other or to the Other that is the world—that, existing independently of the effect of time, might be accessible to human knowledge and worthy to be called love. Such a relation is here evoked only in the subjunctive mood—the mood of surmise. And its possibility is evoked even as certainty of knowledge disappears, with the *passante,* into an endless future: "O toi que j'eusse aimée, ô toi qui le savais!" The alienated encounter, the "rencontre manquée," will be a permanent urban theme of *Le Spleen de Paris.*

> Moi, j'écoute cette journée naître. . . .
>
> C'est d'abord un filtrage . . . comme le bruit d'un barrage. Et c'est aussi le bruit d'un tissage, un départ de navette. . . . Tout à coup, c'est un bruit d'usine, un bruit de manufacture lointaine, un moteur syncopé que coupent les gifles des courroies de transmission.
>
> Est-ce donc cela, la matière du temps? Le bruit même de la machine ronde, encerclé de ciel gris?
>
> (I am listening to the break of day. . . .
>
> First it is a filtering sound . . . like the noise a weir makes. And it is also a weaving noise, a loom starting up. . . . Suddenly it's a factory noise, the sound of distant manufacture, a motor starting and stopping as the transmission cables interfere.
>
> So is this time's materiality? The noise itself of our round machine, circled about by gray sky?)
>
> Léon-Paul Fargue, *Haute solitude*[6]

No longer fetishized as world whose noisiness is denied, the universe assumed by Baudelairean allegory is one in which acknowledgment of noise as, in Fargue's suggestive phrase, the materiality of time becomes the condition of that world's readability. As a consequence, we have seen the idealizing aesthetics of harmony yield to a materialist aesthetics of disorder. The ordinary made alluringly strange through the formal intervention of art has been displaced by a disquietingly inherent strangeness that becomes perceptible on occasion *in* the everyday, an alien dimension that threatens formal constructions such as those of fetish aesthetics with eventual disintegration and decay, just as it reduces human selves to "une espèce de décomposition." The etherealizing atmospherics arising from the idealizing impulse has become materialized as a threatening atmospherics of weather, history, and its modern agent, the crowd, all these manifestations of noise replacing the benevolent agency of the eternal sun. In the absence of a not yet invented scientific meteorology, Baudelaire thus makes the readability of weather a figure of "modern beauty." The object of that readability, though, still remains a form of supernaturalism, albeit a deeply disquieting and pessimistic one; such is the condition of Baudelairean allegory.

Fargue's phrase, *la matière du temps,* is suggestive, however, in that it admits of two interpretations. Does the materiality of time imply the existence of an immaterial dimension of temporality, the eternal? Or does it rather assume the immanence of the material, a state of being without transcendent dimension? And in the latter supposition, what would be the object of time's readability? Can there be a readability of that which has no allegorical depth? The phenomenon of noise, as "la matière du temps," produces both readability and unreadability in equal proportions, for the reason that these are in fact mutually dependent categories. That which is noisy enough to require reading is by definition unreadable to the same degree. Where allegory, then, with its constitutive figures of chiasmic intersection and preteritional devastation, names the *readability* of an urban world defined by the inherited assumptions of supernaturalism and the sacred, that same world of the city, viewed as merely a tangle of intersecting social relations shorn of transcendence—a "fourmillante cité" no longer "pleine de rêves"—poses the problem of noise as a factor of *unreadability*. No longer preternaturally strange, the familiar everyday becomes strangely unknowable by virtue of an *anonymity* that is bafflingly depthless. This is the irony of the Hegelian paradox concerning the unknowability of the familiar, and we shall see that in *Le Spleen de Paris*, urban encounter ceases therefore to have allegorical significance. Instead, it will become an occasion for the acknowledgment of unreadability that is necessarily entailed in the perception of irony. The world of the major prose poems concerned with urban life will be ironic in its structure, in the way that the world of the great poems of "Tableaux parisiens" is allegorical. Such a world is readable, that is, as unreadable.

Alienation will no longer be defined here as unawareness of the *danger* attached to a world governed by the effects of time. It arises instead from the baffling proximity of familiar fellow citizens whom one can know/read no more successfully than one can read/know oneself. As a consequence disalienation—as an awareness of noise in a world without supernaturalist dimension—takes the form of a recognition of *anonymity* as the crucial manifestation of the ironic unreadability of both self and other. And accordingly, the atmosphere of the city ceases to be understood as a readable layer of, as it were, immaterial materiality, mediating between the life of the "fourmillante cité" and a horrifying beyond. It becomes instead something like an impenetrable haze of unreadability—one that now certifies, no less bleakly, the city's abandonment to the hazardous absurdity of a history that seems blind, undirected, and above all, ungovernable, to what Fargue calls "le bruit même de la machine ronde, encerclé de ciel gris."

PART III

Ironic Atmospherics and the Urban Diary

FIVE

Ironic Encounter: The Poetics of Anonymity

If allegory is a figure of readability, offering a glimpse of transcendence—albeit a transcendence of *le Mal*—what are we to make of the clear blue sky that the eponymous swan identifies as the source of its torments? Its cloudless purity, which would seem to suggest the absence of noise, also signifies unambiguously that the answer to the swan's question: "Eau, quand donc pleuvras-tu? Quand tonneras-tu, foudre?" (line 23) is something like: not in the foreseeable future. If there is an atmospherics of readability here, we must identify an atmospherics of fine, clear weather.

For the poetics of *le temps qu'il fait* is at the opposite end of the meteorological scale, here, from the dampness and fog of "Les sept vieillards" or the hurricane in the eye of the *passante,* in which we read an allegory of time in the mode of history (see chapter 4). The swan's suffering arises rather from atmospheric conditions that—very much like the "cieux / Froids et clairs" that preside over the awakening of Labor (lines 14–15)—suggest emptiness, absence, and transparency, even as they promise no end to the suffering of either the Parisian workers or the parched and stranded bird. Understandably, then, the swan appears to "adress[er] des reproches à Dieu" for His abandonment. But also, the God the swan addresses in this way is unresponsive in the way that the sky is itself "cruellement bleu," so that God's unresponsiveness—given Christian belief in His mercy—comes to suggest either that he is absent or that, like the sky, he is withholding a grace that it is in his power to bestow. Either thought is itself a cruel one; and the rhyming of "cruellement bleu" with "Dieu" in the final quatrain of part 1, together with that of "Ovide" and "aride," inevitably suggests the ghost-rhyme "vide" (empty). The idea strongly hinted at in this way is, then, that the emptiness of the sky bespeaks the absence of God from heaven—but an absence experienced by the suffering swan as evidence of an act of cruelty.

In this way "Le Cygne" is consonant with the Baudelairean doctrine of the reign of Evil in the form of a transcendence that governs the stormy atmospherics of allegory. But it suggests also that such a circumstance arises for one of two reasons: it comes about either because God is absent, or else because He is an ironist. For what would it mean to address one's reproaches to an absent God? The swan's reproachful writhing assumes the *presence* of God as tormentor in the clear firmament that simultaneously indicates his apparent absence. It identifies the cruelty of its torture, therefore, as evidence of willful unavailability on the part of a supposedly benign divinity, a withholding of self that has the same structure as the nonparticipation of the subject of speech in an utterance that the subject is for that reason held to proffer ironically. It is the communicational noisiness thus generated—the noise of irony—that restores opacity, uncertainty, and doubt, that is, another form of noise (and one thus capable of generating an atmospherics), to a situation that is only apparently clear, cold, and transparent. For the swan and the divinity do communicate, although they do so wordlessly, the latter by His ironic silence, the other, equally mute, by means of (eloquent) gesture: the open beak, the obsessive shuffling of the "pieds palmés," the neck twisted convulsively, the wings spread like those of the albatross in another, much earlier, Baudelaire poem concerning cruelty, pain, and alienation.[1]

Irony, Anonymity, and the Atmospherics of the Everyday

We might say, then, that if the atmospherics of allegory derives from the noise that generates a readable world, there is also a less readily perceptible atmospherics of transparency—of apparent clarity and purity—that is an atmospherics of irony, corresponding counterintuitively to a certain noisy *un*readability that only counterfeits legibility. This would be the unreadability of a situation rendered *absurd* by the fact that transcendence is to all intents and purposes absent from it, even as it is simultaneously experienced as present, and active to the extent that its absence registers as a form of cruelty, and hence as a manifestation of *le Mal.*

Moreover, these two forms of atmospherics—the allegorical and the ironic—are not at all incompatible, just as readability and unreadability are closely related products of, and responses to, the same phenomenon, which might be interchangeably referred to as noise or as *le Mal.* The absurd unreadability of a world governed, because it is structured ironically, by God's apparent or virtual absence, is the necessary precondition for the readable presence, in the world that is structured allegorically, of an active and powerful agency of evil, hurt, and pain. In these two differing but consonant ways, the universe reveals itself as one from which the ideal—figured by the benign solar divinity of "Je n'ai pas oublié . . . ," for instance—is irrevocably absent.

And the consciousness of *le Mal,* therefore, in the form of spleen or melancholy, is what remains as the only possible response to such a fallen cosmos. It is simply that melancholy, however, has an allegorical mode and an ironic mode, and that these two modes alternate therefore in Baudelaire's late writing in the way that in *Les Fleurs du Mal* the exaltation of the ideal already alternated with the depressive mood of spleen. But the alternation of allegorical melancholy and ironic spleen is figured by the way a simple change of weather can bring about a "ciel cruellement bleu" or alternatively produce the threat of clouds, fog, darkness, and storm (*le temps qu'il fait* acting, as we've seen, as the atmospheric manifestation of *le temps qui passe,* man's eternal Enemy). And Time itself, then, similarly varies in its manifestations between the events of history, to which allegory is a melancholic response, and its secret presence as an unnoticed and unread irony in the unremarkable happenstances of everyday life—those random happenstances out of which, in due course, the events of history themselves emerge, like time condensing into a hurricane, and to which, as they subside, they return their unhappy survivors.

And so, exactly as in the case of allegory and the threat of history in "Tableaux parisiens," the problem of art in *Le Spleen de Paris* will be this: how to make perceptible, to oblivious readers, the secret unreadability of the familiar life of the city, the cruel but transparent irony that haunts the everyday and forms an atmospherics of absence? Can art employ irony on its own behalf and as an agent of disalienation, in the way that allegory functions in "Tableaux parisiens"? These are the stakes of a large and representative number of the prose poems of *Le Spleen,* those in which the social relations that form the purely immanent life of the *civitas* are shown to be governed by the same cruel irony of absence but presence that the swan experiences in its address to the unresponsive heavens.

In these poems, the sign of the ironic inscrutability of such an immanent world—one subject, for the moment, less to history's momentous events, with their intimations of an evil transcendence, than to the kinds of narratable-because-symptomatic encounters that demonstrate the strange unreadability of what is familiar and taken for granted—will be the *anonymity* that is as much a marker of the urban crowd as is its multiplicity. In the verse of the "Tableaux parisiens," the anonymity of, say, a "mendiante rousse," the "petites vieilles," or "les aveugles" is a phenomenon apparently taken for granted and not examined—useful even, when (quite exceptionally) poems like "Je n'ai pas oublié . . ." and "La servante au grand coeur . . ." are left untitled—that is, nameless—with a view to protecting their private significance.[2] But in *Le Spleen*, anonymity becomes an active factor of estrangement, one that results from the ironic inaccessibility to knowledge of that which is nevertheless recognizable and familiar, and more particularly from the unreadability of the ordinary faces in the street that one may see, simultaneously present and absent, every day. An anonymity/unreadability that includes the people, not excluding oneself, with whom one may live in the closest proximity.

Titles like "L'Étranger," "Le mauvais vitrier," "Le vieux saltimbanque," "Le Joujou du pauvre," "Les Yeux des pauvres," "Le Joueur généreux," "Assommons les pauvres" ("The Stranger," "The Bad Glazier," "The Old Street Performer," "The Poor Person's Toy," "The Eyes of the Poor," "The Generous Gambler," "Let's Beat Up the Poor"), or even the nickname title "Mademoiselle Bistouri" (Miss Scalpel), are indicative, in this way, of the everyday ironies that are generated by the phenomenon of anonymity in a world become immanent by virtue of God's own ironic abandonment of humans to a world of their own devising: the artificial environment of the city. Here the swan's relation to the divinity is reproduced in the relations of a purely social world in which insight into human particularity and personhood is blocked by the familiarity and ready recognizability of generalizing categories relating to physical characteristics, social status, or one's trade or profession.

Where encounter is the key concept of the allegorical verse poems of "Tableaux parisiens" (and chiasmus their most significant figural model), it is the word *croisement,* rather—a word suggestive of an encounter without meeting or without contact—that Baudelaire deploys in the famous letter to Arsène Houssaye that serves as preface to most modern editions of *Le Spleen.* And where allegorical encounter has the exceptional character, the singularity of an event, the crisscrossings that the prose poems sample are characterized by their frequency and hence banality ("la fréquentation des villes énormes," "[le] croisement de leurs innombrables rapports" [*OC* 1:276; the frequentation of enormous cities, the intersections of their innumerable relationships]). They are endowed in this way with the familiarity that both engenders and makes invisible their strangeness, producing in this way a potential for irony. For nothing passes unnoticed more easily than an irony; yet it is their irony—the Hegelian irony of the familiar that cannot be known precisely because it is so familiar—that makes these nameless *croisements* so impenetrably strange. Baudelaire's project will therefore consist of producing an effect of disalienation by enacting in his writing this ironic unreadability that is inherent, although generally invisible, in the familiar phenomenon of the urban *croisement.*

This was not, at least officially, the project of flâneur writing as the genre existed at the time; because they are symptomatic, Baudelaire's anecdotes are closer in their spirit to another journalistic genre, that of the *fait divers* or brief item of news. Flâneur writing is generally credited with mitigating, to some extent, the effects of proximate distancing, that is of alienation, that arose in the nineteenth century as a consequence of sharp class and economic differences, on the one hand, and of urban crowding—a new and unaccustomed population density—on the other. Supposedly the educated classes, who could read, gained insight into the lives of the laboring or unemployed urban masses from the entertaining descriptions published by the mediating flâneurs. But from a Baudelairean point of view such "insight" is purely illusory. It can only reinforce the existing alienation of city dwellers by encouraging them in the illusion that it is both possible and easy for them to understand one another.

The *fait divers*, in contrast, has to do with the way anonymous lives that are normally a matter of indifference and casual ignorance can become newsworthy. Notable things can happen to people of no account, those who remain anonymous, as it were, even when they are named. But the twist introduced by the anecdotes of *Le Spleen* will be that the effects of anonymity, when people find themselves relating to one another (if relating is the word) on one of the innumerable occasions of *croisement* that are presented by city life, can themselves become a matter of interest, and an object of scrutiny. And this is precisely because people turn out, despite their easy recognizability (and indeed because of it), to be so ironically inscrutable, and hence unknowable, each to the other. The matter of the anecdotal prose poems that form a large part of *Le Spleen* consists of an investigation, then, of that mutual inscrutability and unknowability, on the occasion of a chance *croisement* that turns out to have symptomatic significance, like a *fait divers*.

However, these occasions are not narrated in the manner of typical flâneur or *fait divers* journalism. Intrigued by the problematic encounter that forms the poem's happenstance subject matter, the reader is drawn into a narrative that itself duplicates, for that reader, the experience of ironic encounter. The act of reading becomes less an occasion of comprehension than it is itself a *croisement,* a frustrated engagement with a text that proves inscrutable. In "Tableaux parisiens," the reader's disalienation depends on an effect of *mimesis,* the poem that recounts its narrator's shattering experience of disalienation functioning, ideally, as if it was itself, for the reader, some sort of allegorical statue. Its narrative structure—the before and after, centered on a disalienating event, of "Les sept vieillards" or "À une passante," say—substitutes for the exploration of a statue from different points of view that Baudelaire describes in the *Salon de 1859,* so that the reader is led to mime, as it were, the evolving experience of the narrator's own becoming disalienated. In the prose poems in question, however, the effect of ironic unreadability that produces disalienation is an effect of the act of reading itself, the textual irony placing the reader in a position of unbearable thirst strikingly comparable with the suffering of the swan, since it is a thirst for there to be, discoverable within the text, a site of authoritative and reliable meaning that proves to be cruelly lacking.

Vainly scrutinizing the "ciel ironique et cruellement bleu" of a text that is apparently transparent but proves to be infinitely noisy, such a reader duplicates the swan's entreaties to God as he or she vainly searches the text for evidence of the presence of a controlling "author"—even one assumed to be cruelly and ingeniously unavailable to scrutiny. And such a search is likely to conclude in an assumption of authorial absence, or at least anonymity. The textual subject, if such there be, proves to be lacking—and to be lacking in particular the transcendent knowledge, of himself and of others, that might confer on him a status other than that of supreme ironist. It is, of course, precisely this demotion of the author, the loss of aura or halo effect to which he is subject when exposed to the "moving chaos" of the noise-filled city street, that is at issue in "Perte d'auréole."

As figures of unreadability, then, the becoming transparent of the urban atmosphere is of a piece with the becoming blank of the textual subject and the becoming anonymous of the city poet, no longer a numinous figure but undistinguishable henceforth from the crowd of nameless others. In Baudelaire's *oeuvre,* it is the cruelty of irony that thus comes to displace, albeit without replacing, the quality of supernaturalism that, according to the famous *fusée* (*OC* 1:658), is its indispensable other. And what remains is the experience of noise.

Accommodating to Noise: "Perte d'auréole"

"Perte d'auréole" is mildly ironic in its tone, but as a kind of fable or parable its most immediate and pertinent relation to the practice of irony in *Le Spleen* lies in its exploration of the eternal Baudelaire problem of the relation of the poet, and of poetry, to the phenomenon of noise—that is of entropy—and to the motor of entropy that is time. For textual noise is the verbal manifestation of irony in the way that material disorder, disharmony, and decay are the work of time; and both pose the problem of poetic identity that attaches to the becoming anonymous of the poet, his loss of aura.

The germ of the anecdote is related in a *fusée* (*OC* I:659), where it is significantly positioned immediately following a note concerning supernaturalism and the "symbolic" role of the ordinary:

> Dans certains états d'âme presque surnaturels, la profondeur de la vie se révèle tout entière dans le spectacle, si ordinaire qu'il soit, qu'on a sous les yeux. Il en devient le symbole.

> (In certain almost supernatural states of mind, life's depth is revealed entirely in the scene before one's eyes, however ordinary it may be. It becomes the symbol of that depth.)

The word *symbole* is new; but in this late jotting we are in the world of fetish aesthetics that preceded the allegorical understanding of time and history as manifestations of *le Mal.* This is evidence, if it is needed, that Baudelaire does not readily abandon any understanding he has once had. But what follows this note is a summary account of an imagined accident on one of the new boulevards, but with an outcome significantly different from that related in "Perte d'auréole":

> Comme je traversais le boulevard, et comme je mettais un peu de précipitation à éviter les voitures, mon auréole s'est détachée et est tombée dans la boue du macadam. J'eus heureusement le temps de la ramasser; . . .

> (As I was crossing the boulevard and hopping about a bit to avoid the carriages, my halo slipped off and fell to the muddy asphalt. Fortunately I had time to retrieve it . . .)

In the context of the idealist supernaturalism of the immediately preceding *fusée,* not only is the dropped "auréole" the sign of poetic aura, quickly picked up and restored to its rightful place on the poet's brow, but also the incident of its loss troubles the poet in this version: it constitutes a "mauvais présage," he says, an evil omen; and he remains troubled by it all day. There is no hint of the equanimity the auraless poet will display about its permanent loss in the developed version published in *Le Spleen.*

But then, and especially when it is read in the context of this *fusée* version, both his equanimity over the loss of his "auréole" in the *Spleen* version and the heavy irony with which he expresses that equanimity begin to sound more than a little forced, and hence insincere:

> je pense avec joie que quelque mauvais poète la ramassera et s'en coiffera impudemment. Faire un heureux, quelle joie!
>
> (I reflect joyfully that some bad poet will pick it up and impudently wear it on his head. Such joy it is to make someone happy!)

This assignment to a "mauvais poète" of the action of stopping to pick the "aureole" out of the "fange du macadam"—that is, of what, in the *fusée* version, was his own reaction—suggests a degree of bluster in his assertion, and hence a certain dubiousness concerning the "mauvais lieu" (low dive) in which his acquaintance has recognized him: "Je me trouve bien ici" (I'm comfortable here), he asserts. This hardly suggests that he is genuinely at ease, either in his sordid surroundings or in his new, auraless, status (might they not together imply, or be taken to imply, that it is he who is the "mauvais poète"?). So it is worth specifying what Baudelaire's contemporaries would certainly have known, that "la fange du macadam" (in the *fusée* "la boue du macadam") is a euphemistic reference to the horse droppings and/or raw sewage trickling like a rivulet down the proud, new, Haussmannian boulevard.

The available options, then, for a poet whose aura has fallen victim to the conditions of urban modernity, are either to sport a damaged and excrement-stained aura like a bad poet, or to go auraless in practicing some new kind of poetry of the ordinary, and of the ordinary shorn of its "symbolic" relation to "la profondeur de la vie," the supernatural. The choice is not an easy one. But it begins to account, perhaps, for what is in effect the "third way"—the way of ironic abstention, or absence, on the poet's part, from his own text—that will be the marker of the prose poems of urban life in *Le Spleen*: a kind of denial of self by means of an actively *assumed* anonymity that supplies a transparent, clear-blue-sky, *textual* atmosphere as a substitute for the *auréole* no longer available to the poet in person. At the price of becoming an anonymous presence in his own text, the poet will abdicate his personal aura in favor of the noise of textual irony.

But in "Perte d'auréole" this recourse to anonymity is not available to him, since at the outset he was *recognized* by his acquaintance, and recognized in a "mauvais lieu" (doubtless a brothel, or perhaps a low-class drinking establishment). Recognized, that is, not just as some nameless member of the class of poets (as one might say "a workman" or "a beggar"), but *in propria persona*: recognized as a specific, namable individual known to exercise the profession of poet. "Eh! quoi! Vous ici mon cher? Vous dans un mauvais lieu!" (What! You here old chap? You in a low dive!). So, he blusters. And it is against that specificity and namability that, in an important group of prose poems concerning ordinary, unredeemed urban life, Baudelaire deploys the resources of authorial anonymity that are offered, as an intimation of divine inscrutability, by the practice of textual irony. Irony will solve the problem of remaining active as a poet without being recognizable in the poem, as the wearer of an *auréole* would be.

In this respect, "Perte d'auréole" offers something like a negative key to such a poetic practice, then. But it does so because, as a very late text (dating presumably from 1865 and unpublished in Baudelaire's lifetime), it represents also a point of culmination in respect of the poet's ongoing struggle, post-1848–51, to deploy the harmonizing resources of verse against the realities—extension, distance, difference, discordancy, noise, and, in short, history—of time the Enemy. Abandoning now "les hasards de la rime" ("Le Soleil"), Baudelaire's turn to prose takes a decisive step, one of which—in the prose poem—the poet figure's abandonment of his aura in the mud is the definitive symbol. The question now becomes how to maintain a diction recognizably poetic, without recourse to the rhythmic and rhyming resources of verse that constitutes the traditional poet's claim to a new, if tarnished, *auréole*.

In the terms of the 1862 letter to Houssaye—terms symptomatically formulated in the contradictory manner of oxymoron—such a discourse would be "une prose poétique, musicale sans rythme et sans rime" (*OC* 1:275); and such a form of prose would be capable, also oxymoronically, of "translating" into poetry "le cri strident du *Vitrier*" (the Glazier's strident cry). This, then, would be a poetry whose problematic musicality, rather than opposing noise, would arise from its capacity, as a kind of compromise formation, to accommodate to noise's reality, as demanded by the conditions of urban life: "la fréquentation des villes énormes," with "le croisement de leurs innombrables rapports." "Trouver une langue" (A language to be found), Rimbaud was to write a little later, confirming Baudelaire's conviction that a poetry of modernity must entail forms of language and modes of writing that, far from being hostile to the glazier's ear-splitting stridency, are attuned to such discordancy.[3] And it is the practice of irony, I am suggesting, that for Baudelaire performs this "miracle" of translating—in the sense of introducing—noise into a textual music; irony that densifies and makes opaque a text otherwise transparent in its prosaic ordinariness. The irony, for example, that informs the letter to Houssaye itself.[4]

Two familiar motifs associated with the thematics of time and of noise come to a sort of culmination, then, in the final abandonment of hostilities that is recorded in "Perte d'auréole"—less a truce, it seems, than an accommodation to the inevitable. One is that of the street as artificial river; the other that of the poet's "fantasque escrime" as he struggles in the street with "les hasards de la rime." The street as a river that one steps *down* into—the verb in French would be *descendre*—becomes the site of an actual fall, that of the "auréole." Already a swollen stream in "Les sept vieillards" (line 7: "une rivière accrue"), the muddy boulevard is now a sight of nightmarish uproar, a "chaos mouvant où la mort arrive au galop" (a living chaos in which death comes at you at a gallop), as the flood of traffic (totally unregulated as it was in Baudelaire's day) descends from all directions on the haptic pedestrian attempting to cross. The image is that of a swollen and tempestuous river. And the poet's hops and struggles as he attempts to maintain his balance—"Je sautillais dans la rue" (I was hopping about in the street)—take the "fantasque escrime" of "Le Soleil" to a new extreme, and one with a drastic outcome as, "dans un mouvement brusque" (making a sudden movement), he loses his *auréole*. The descent of the poet into the street, begun at the turning point marked by "Le Soleil," has ended in ignominious defeat. The *auréole* lies in the repulsive filth of the street; and the damage being done, there is no point in attempting to repair it. "Je n'ai pas eu le courage de la ramasser" (I didn't have the heart to pick it up).

Giving up the struggle against time and noise in this way, the poet remains a poet, however. There is no sign that he has abandoned his vocation along with his lost aura—only that his conception of poetic identity has altered: "Vous seul m'avez reconnu" (You alone have recognized me), he tells his interlocutor.

> Je peux maintenant me promener incognito, faire des actions basses, et me livrer à la crapule, comme les simples mortels. Et me voici, tout semblable à vous, comme vous le voyez.

> (I can walk about incognito now, do vile things, and revel in dissoluteness, just like ordinary mortals. And here I am, just like you, as you see.)

He does not indicate here the strictly poetic advantages of anonymity that reside in the practice of irony. Rimbaud, for example, who will remember the idea of *encrapulement* as the way to a new conception of poetic calling, seems also to have read the poet's anonymity here as a sign that poetry can work, less for the glorification of an individual lyric subject than as a *communitarian* practice, to be shared with "d'autres horribles travailleurs" (other horrible workers). And this *croisement,* in a low dive, of an anonymous poet with his equally anonymous, or at least unnamed, friend is certainly suggestive, understood as a *mise en abyme* of the conditions of an auraless poetic practice, of a working out, under radically transformed conditions, of a new kind of *entente* between poet and reader, reader and poet.

For Baudelaire, in any case—assuming "Baudelaire" to be the name of this newly anonymous convert to a poetics of noise—the die is cast. He has stumbled, literally, into an understanding of poetic practice that implies effacement, discretion, restraint: an abandonment of all forms of poetic resistance—that is, of "heroism"—in the face of the conditions of modern life.[5] Rejecting his friend's suggestion that he advertise to get his lost aura back, he seems determined instead to pursue his avocation in a new and noise-friendly, rather than noise-adversative, way. The Poet's new effacement—as no longer what his friend calls the "buveur de quintessences" (drinker of quintessences) and the "mangeur d'ambroisie" (ambrosia eater)—implies a more modest and, as it were, lowercase practice of the poetic. And this, I am arguing, will be one in which the anonymity of the lyric self, as a necessary condition of participation in the *croisements* of ordinary, anonymous people that are the characteristic mode of alienated urban sociality, becomes also the condition of an act of disalienation. Not the disalienation of the Poet that we witness in the allegorical verse poems; that is now a given. But that of the reader, who will be drawn into a disalienating encounter—not just a *croisement,* but a genuine engagement—with the opaque transparency, the intriguing and baffling unreadability, and the cruelty, if you will, of textual irony. That is, with anonymity itself—the loss of individual personhood—made readable though the experience of textual unreadability.

Shattering Illusions: "Le mauvais vitrier"

If the irony the reader encounters reproduces that entailed in the urban *croisements* which form the subject matter of so many poems, those encounters themselves fall into different categories:

1. The meeting may be between or among figures anonymous to one another in that, although the *mésentente* that separates them partially or wholly escapes recognition on the part of the participants, it is perceptible to a thoughtful reader, who may draw appropriate generalizing conclusions. "Les yeux des pauvres" is an example of this category.
2. Alternatively the *mésentente* may be experienced by a participant as a baffled sense of an other's opacity to reading, as in "Mademoiselle Bistouri."
3. Finally, social differences, notably those of class and wealth, readily generate irrational acts of violence, as in "Le Gâteau," "Assommons les pauvres," or "Le mauvais vitrier." The poems in this last category are frequently understood as ironic parables; and contemporary criticism tends to read them in

> relation to the social and political theory of the mid-nineteenth century, notably that of Proudhon, and to detect in them echoes of the disastrously divisive events of 1848–51.[6]

The narrator of "Le mauvais vitrier," however, is fully aware of the irrationality of the impulse that prompts him to attack the eponymous *vitrier*. He speaks of "une impulsion mystérieuse," "une force irrésistible," "une si folle énergie," "ces crises et ces élans" (a mysterious prompting, an irresistible force, such mad energy, these crises and sudden impulses) that govern his behavior and lead him into speculation about a malicious Demon supposedly exercising its "absurdes volontés" (absurd wishes) on him, as its hapless agent. He even interrupts his narrative after he has finally embarked on it, with a long parenthetical afterthought concerning the theological and medical categories—satanism or hysteria—that might account for his spasmodic outbursts. In short, he reveals himself to us as self-centered and self-indulgent—more concerned with his own sensations and the ins and outs of his psyche than with his victim whose stock-in-trade—that is, his livelihood—he has smashed for the thrill of it.

Readers are thus led to understand the narrator figure as the real protagonist of the poem, and the focus of its attention, treating the victim as a secondary character. They may identify him as an authorial self-portrait, for example, or speculate in turn on his social class (a typical bourgeois?) or the aesthetic impulse ("La vie en beau! La vie en beau!") that leads him to attack the *vitrier*. But this is to miss something, thanks to Baudelaire's strategic obfuscation; they enjoy the pun when the narrator lays claim to an "action d'éclat," a "smashing" exploit, but may not reflect, for example, on the possible symbolic significance of the glazier's stock-in-trade itself: the windowpane or *vitre* that his flowerpot-dropping assailant accuses of being insufficiently life enhancing. They may also fail to reflect on the valency attached to the height from which the destructive flowerpot is launched, in relation to the association of the glazier with the street and with the noise that so irritates the fastidious observer from above when he incautiously throws open his window:

> j'ouvris la fenêtre, hélas! [There follows the paragraph-long parenthesis devoted to self-diagnosis. Then:] La première personne que je vis dans la rue, ce fut un vitrier dont le cri perçant, discordant monta jusqu'à moi à travers la lourde atmosphère parisienne.
>
> (I opened the window, alas! . . . The first person I saw in the street was a glazier whose shrill, discordant cry came up to me through the heavy/sultry Parisian atmosphere.)
>
> (*OC* 1:286)

What joins and divides the upstairs dweller and the denizen of the street is the phenomenon of atmosphere, "heavy" with implications, here, as well as with dust, smoke and noise (unless of course it refers to atmospheric pressure, and the oppressiveness that foretells a storm). The history I traced in chapter 2—from the sun-refracting *vitre* of "Je n'ai pas oublié . . ." to the protective, garret-height windowpane of "Paysage" and its abandonment in favor of a poetry of the street in direct rivalry with the sun—is implicit in "Le mauvais vitrier" and active in the discordancy the narrator encounters in opening his window to the urban scene: he who combines in his person psychological noise and the desire for an idealizing aesthetics of harmony and beauty. For the history in question is, of course, that of a search for an alternative, be it in rhyming allegory or in prosaic irony, to exactly the sort of fetish aesthetics that the narrator, with his preference for "vitres de couleur" (colored panes) over transparency and his desire for "la vie en beau" (life beautified), clearly subscribes to. Can it be then—in light of this Baudelairean background that forms the "heavy" atmosphere of the poem—that the ungainly *vitrier,* whose stock-in-trade makes his ascent up the stairs hazardous, who stumbles when pushed by the narrator and finally falls in a shatter of glass, is as much an inheritor of "Le soleil" and its "fantasque escrime" as is the auraless narrator of "Perte d'auréole"? And, as such, a figure of irony therefore, in the way that the narrator functions as a figure for the persistent, albeit irrational, appeal of an antagonistic aesthetics of fetish?

If so, the contradictory aesthetic trends that form the dilemma of an art of modernity are mapped here onto the brittle class relations of post-1848 and Second Empire France, and embodied in the narrative of a property owner (we know that he possesses a flower pot and the strategic balcony from which to drop it) who picks a fight with a proletarian over panes of glass. Irony readily deflates the idealist pretensions of an aesthetics of fetishism, with its pseudosupernaturalism, much as the call for "verres de couleur" mocks the sorry transparency of the *vitrier*'s merchandise, clouded as it is with the air bubbles that, in the days of "Je n'ai pas oublié . . ." cooperated with the sun to fetishistic effect. The two, in short, have much in common, beginning with the status they share as artifices of language or tropes. They are fraternal enemies; the (fake) depth and dimensionality of the fetish object—its atmosphere or aura—is of a piece with the (deceptive) transparency, but real opacity, of the ironic subject. And the readability of the one, the unreadability of the other, have in common their relation to noise: a relation corrective in the case of fetish, which seeks to deny it, but collusive in the case of irony, which affirms the reality of noise as constitutive.

Each the other's other, the two are fraternal enemies, then, and their engagement in "Le mauvais vitrier," with its reminiscence of June 1848, has much in common with the fierce fight of "Le Gâteau" ("une guerre parfaitement fratricide" [*OC* 1:299; a perfectly fratricidal struggle] over a bit of bread), but equally with the rich child and the poor child in "Le Joujou du pauvre," united in their fascination with a caged rat, who laugh "fraternellement, avec des dents d'une égale blancheur" (*OC* 1:305 fraternally, and showing teeth equally white). Baudelaire is rewriting here the stations of his own aesthetic evolution (the fetish aesthetics of a benevolent, then malevolent, supernaturalism; the turn to irony and to prose), but doing so not at all as a history of progress—a dialectic, say, that would admit of sublation.[7] Rather it might be thought of as a kind of unresolvable family bickering among the various possible responses available to art, given the conditions of modern life—conditions that include the inescapability of artifice, but also the "highs" and "lows" of aesthetic options (in the present case the fakery of tinted glass versus the pseudotransparency of ordinary glass) as well as of social life (the fraternal warfare of rich and poor, working class and bourgeoisie).

For conflict—social, political, or aesthetic—is as much a consequence of a society's lost access to the natural as is the recourse to artifice. If fetish aesthetics responds to the lost natural by inventing a form of illusory desirability, melancholy turns back toward the past in order to lament the lost natural in the form of allegories of history, while irony in its turn responds with acerbity to the evidence of alienation that lies in the unresolvable conflicts and tensions of the everyday here and now that is something like modernity's substitute for the natural. In this respect, what distinguishes the three aesthetic options that together define Baudelaire's *oeuvre* much less as a site of unity than as a noisy and disharmonious entity, a site of difference and dispersion, is their relation to the question of modernity understood as an experience of alienation from the (supposedly) natural. For, to put it in Baudelairean terms, they each pose the question of art as an agency of "la conscience dans le mal," that is, of disalienation.

If the everyday life of the city deprives its citizens of awareness concerning the true conditions of their existence by virtue of its very familiarity, art can contribute to their alienation through the illusions produced by nostalgic compensating mechanisms that produce objects of false, because fetishistic, desire: "la vie en beau." Alternatively, it can deploy the techniques of allegory, relying on the reader's identification with a narrator who relates the experience of his own disalienating encounter with the actual uncanniness of the apparently ordinary and familiar, the depth of history inherent in the here and now. Or finally, by means of the unreadability effect that arises in the presence of textual irony, it can produce an effect of readerly disidentification or estrangement, the reader experiencing the tormenting unavailability to scrutiny, the anonymity of the subject of the text, as opposed to its ostensible narrator. This is the effect of ironic distancing—not dissimilar from the Brechtian *Verfremdungseffekt*—that the reader of *Le Spleen de Paris* so frequently encounters in the poems (such as "Le mauvais vitrier") that relate cases of urban *croisement.*

Disalienation is not freedom from the comfortable illusions of alienation, however. Rather, as I pointed out earlier, it is an awareness of the strength of their inescapable grip on modern consciousness, including the disalienated consciousness. The flowerpot of "Le mauvais vitrier" that shatters the kind of fetishizing illusions that Baudelaire too once attached to the windowpane, does so—as far as the narrator's view of things goes—precisely in the name of the comforts procured by such illusionism. And if the narrator's earlier action of throwing open his window to the noisy world of the street, together with the heavy urban atmosphere it embodies, is a gesture to all intents and purposes disalienating in its effect, that same narrator immediately repents of his thoughtlessness and, the narrative suggests, in due course takes revenge by means of his act of aggression at the expense of the hapless glazier. To shatter illusions, as irony so effectively does, is not necessarily to abolish them, therefore; while to become aware of them as illusions, through disalienating gestures like throwing open a window, is also to realize the power they exert.

So if there is a germ of truth to be gained from "Le mauvais vitrier," it might be summed up in the dual applicability of the word *mauvais* in the title. As a disalienating agent, the stridency of the glazier's cry is *mauvais* in the sense of inadequate, while as a supplier of comfortable illusion he also fails miserably, and is accordingly punished by the narrator's act of vengeance. Illusions can be shattered, but it is also illusory to shatter them, since the desire that prompts them is not thereby abolished, or even assuaged. The world is noisy, whether one is aware of it or not.

The prevalence of irony in *Le Spleen* has been recognized since the work of Sonya Stephens, which was itself preceded by Marie Maclean's exploration of the prose poems' narrative performativity.[8] My emphasis, accordingly, has been on the significance of textual irony as an agency of readerly estrangement: the work of disalienation. However, there is another irony at work in the collection, one unintended by the author and purely circumstantial in its origin, an irony independent of the ironist. For the surviving evidence indicates that Baudelaire's intention was to group his prose poems into categories that would together form an ordered collection of interrelated poems under a unifying title, as he had done in *Les Fleurs du Mal*. At the trial of the verse collection for "outrage aux moeurs" (moral indecency), his defense had been that "un livre doit être jugé dans son ensemble" (a book must be judged as a whole); and the sincerity of this stance was demonstrated by the pain he experienced when the carefully balanced "ensemble" of *Les Fleurs* was destroyed by the banning of a number of poems. But it is also evident from the surviving notes that at the time when his work was interrupted by his stroke, followed by his death, he had been able neither to conceive of a suitable structure for the prose poems nor to invent a satisfactory title, a problem exacerbated, furthermore, by the fact that new ideas for poems were still constantly occurring to him. It was as if the book was, not accidentally, but constitutively unfinished. The posthumous edition of 1869 prepared by Asselineau and Banville appeared, then, with a neutral title: *Petits Poèmes en prose,* and seems randomly ordered; if perchance new poems were discovered, there would be no structural reason not to add them to a later edition.[9]

The unintended irony, then, is that in this way a new genre was inadvertently invented, one that, I will propose in chapter 6, has characteristics of *constitutive* disorder and unfinishedness that make it uniquely compatible with the phenomenon of urban noise as well as the ongoing temporality of which, as a manifestation of entropy, such noise is evidence. This noisy genre I will call the *urban diary*: and it is the paradoxical character of a *poet's* urban diary as a noise-friendly genre that I think deserves attention. For genre is a device that conventionally works to facilitate relatively noise-free interactions: in the case of a literary genre, the interaction of a writing and a reading.[10] But what does it take, and what does it mean—what kind of generic interaction is mediated—when a genre seeks to make readable, as an atmospherics of textuality, the unreadable noise generated by the life of a city? Does such a genre generate the kind of reading-writing interaction that, following Baudelaire's hint, might be called a *croisement,* a meeting at cross-purposes?

Or can it be thought to mediate something akin to a genuine engagement?

Some light is thrown on this problem by "Le mauvais vitrier." For what is this narrative if not itself a story of cross-purposes provoked by a deliberate genre infringement? The genre of commercial transaction, understood by the unwary glazier as facilitating the sale of a pane of glass, is hijacked on an irrational impulse and becomes something else instead: something like a cruel practical joke. What the glazier took for a contract turns out not to be *the* contract. Whether he himself gets the point of this—perceiving (a) that he has been tricked, and (b) that the real genre in which he has involuntarily participated is that of the practical joke—is immaterial. A careful reader can see that a genre becomes noisy as a function of its relation (of difference and similarity) to other genres: and that the unreadability generated by genre uncertainty—a form of noise, like the bewilderment presumably experienced by the glazier—is a question of misrecognition. Understood otherwise, that unreadability becomes the prose poem's point, its generic *raison d'être.*

Le Spleen de Paris is no practical joke, but it may function a little like one, generically speaking. I mean that to read the collection in expectation of the kind of flâneur writing that understands itself as mitigating the effects of urban alienation, or alternatively as a subtly ordered ensemble of texts in the manner of *Les Contemplations* or *Les Fleurs du Mal,* is to be baffled as the consequence of a misprision. For it is precisely the collection's *failure* to become an ensemble, its alienating cultivation of disunity that, disalienatingly, it offers us to be read. Unreadability is the generic feature that constitutes its point and makes it readable. The genre that subserves the representation of everyday urban temporality as the atmosphere of everyday life will necessarily be one that is itself generically noisy and uncertain, a *bricolage,* like a practical joke, of other genres subserving moments that pass and change.

SIX

“La forme d’une ville”: The Urban Diary

> O douleur! ô douleur! Le Temps mange la vie,
> Et l’obscur Ennemi qui nous ronge le coeur
> Du sang que nous perdons croît et se fortifie!
> (Time consumes existence, pain by pain,
> and the hidden enemy that gnaws our heart
> feeds on the blood we lose, and flourishes!)
>
> L’Ennemi

The Baudelairean thematics of encounter (or of *croisement*) does not exhaust the poet’s sense of the secret presence, in modern life, of *le Mal*: time, disorder, noise, and, in short, the Enemy. The history that manifests itself in events, be they major or minor events, has a much less spectacular double in the secret, but similarly preteritional, passage of time that underlies the apparent stability of what is now called the everyday.

For what feels like an enduring present is actually the chaotic becoming-future of the past and becoming-past of the future that defines a reality of incessant change, perpetual entropic flux. Here, then, is a parasitic phenomenon so discreet as to defy literary representation through purely rhetorical devices such as allegory and irony. Its representation entails a kind of literary *bricolage*, one whose outcome, I want to claim, is the invention of new generic modes, of which Baudelaire's prose poem collection as it was published in 1869 is an instructive example. For it is not the representation of supposedly eternal verities but the becoming-readable of time itself as the secret atmosphere of urban life that defines the function of modes of writing and understandings of writing's mission that thereby identify themselves as modern.[1]

Baudelaire's initial response to the reality of time and noise had been, as we observed, to employ poetic form as an idealizing and hence fetishistic mode of denial. It was only following the bitter disillusionment of 1848–51, after which harmonian constructions of such a kind could only appear (self-)deceptive and illusory, that there began his long struggle to invent an alternative poetics, one that would be capable of acknowledging, through the resources of allegory and irony, and of drawing attention to, the dangerous reality of atmospheric noise. The urgency of such a disalienating project arose, in particular, from Baudelaire's conviction that the phenomenon that is today designated, more or less neutrally (or at least scientifically), by the term *entropy* represented in reality a force of metaphysical danger, a sinister form of sacrality that threatened humanity with harm and destruction. In Baudelaire's later years, Joseph de Maistre's emphasis on original sin became for him the prevailing sense of a malevolent scourge, one unleashed, under an ironic and seemingly disengaged sky, by the long history of humanity's turning away from nature in favor of the artifice inherent, since Troy, in urban civilization, with its consequent fall into time and noise. The melancholy of "Le Cygne," as we saw, arises from this sense of a fall into history initiating the West's lengthy decline, a fall and decline of which allegory is a product, and at the same time the means by which it is revealed.

That Baudelaire was fully conscious of the paradoxical character of an aesthetic project that entailed the making poetic of noise, poetry's other, is evidenced by his consciousness of *poiesis* as a "fantasque escrime": a somewhat desperate and fatally unsystematic, improvisational practice. I will distinguish now between rhetorical practices that *signify* noise, and formal practices that *embody* it, as a textual characteristic. Allegory and irony introduce noise as the object of rhetorical practices of figuration.[2] But as a formalizing intervention, one that takes as its very material the force of disintegration that reduces the systematic and the constructed to formlessness and ruin, the poetic enterprise inevitably entails also, quite independently of purely rhetorical solutions like allegory or irony, another form of *bricolage*. This would be a search for new genres that might be capable of naturalizing and making readable the dynamics of change, erosion, and disorder at work in the textual material itself. Of such a consequence, Baudelaire may well have been at least half-conscious; for the phenomenon of genre exists precisely to facilitate different kinds of communicational interactions—in the case of literary genres the interactions of reading with writing—by activating shared presuppositions concerning the nature and purpose of such exchanges.

Writing, that is, can become (readable as) noisy—by which I mean resistant to the "normal," harmonizing, and sense-making practice of reading—only in the context of a generic understanding of what might constitute "noisy" writing as, say, a literary practice or mode. And Baudelaire's project of a writing of noise, necessitated by the conditions of modernity, could become *recognized* as such—that is, as readable—only by seeking out, or creating, readers whose own repertoire of generic expectations might include the possibility of such an enterprise as a formal manifestation of formlessness. So it is significant that the 1862 letter to Houssaye that stands at the head of most modern editions of the prose poem collection as if it were a kind of preface shows Baudelaire to have been reflecting, precisely, on the *formal* problematics of an urban poetics, and on its *generic* preconditions.

Formally speaking, these, it seems, would entail in Baudelaire's thinking the invention of a poetry in prose. Generically they would also adapt the inherited conventions of lyric expression to the vagaries of urban consciousness:

> Qui est celui . . . qui n'a pas . . . rêvé le miracle d'une prose poétique . . . assez souple et assez heurtée pour s'adapter aux mouvements lyriques de l'âme, aux ondulations de la rêverie, aux soubresauts de la conscience?
>
> (Who is he . . . who has not . . . dreamed of the miracle of a poetic prose . . . sufficiently adaptable and sufficiently abrupt to be adapted to the soul's lyrical flights, the undulations of reverie, and the somersaults of conscience?)
>
> (*OC* 1:275–76)

Baudelaire, it seems, is proposing here a generic *détournement* of the lyric genre by claiming the hypothetical existence of a community of dreamers supposed to be already conscious of the necessity of such a radical adaptation. For the apparently impossible enterprise (cf. "miracle") of a poetics of noise, as a "making" devoted precisely to the principle of unmaking or dissolution, becomes feasible precisely when, and if, it can be described, and recognized, in relation to already existing genre understandings; and this is the case even if such understandings (those of the lyric in Baudelaire's thinking) are radically violated, and—as a consequence of precisely that violation of expectations—introduce noise into the genre system itself. For, as "Le mauvais vitrier" demonstrates, the violation of a genre has generic implications of its own, and can thus bring new, and previously unthought, significations into play. In the way that a presumed *transaction* can be hijacked in such a way as to become a *practical joke*—or better, perhaps, the *malicious ambush* of an unsuspecting victim—the lyric can lend itself to what then passes as constituting something previously considered antinomic to the lyric: a poetics of noise.

Something of that kind must, I think, have been Baudelaire's insight. But what I want to propose is that, in the actual event, "his" generic invention in *Le Spleen de Paris* turned out to be less a radical transformation of lyricism, in the way that the poet himself had apparently intended, than an accidental adaptation, owing to the author's death and the posthumous intervention of his editors, of existing practices of collective flâneur writing; and that these collective practices—by definition unsystematic and uncoordinated—came to constitute in this way an authorial project, attributable to "Charles Baudelaire."[3] This project I will call a poet's urban diary; and in its accidental appropriation of the noisiness of collective writing, such an invention, I suggest, came to represent a significant early site of the writerly "death of the author," in that phrase's Barthesian sense.[4] So my own titular appropriation of the famous parenthesis of "Le Cygne" (applying the phrase "la forme d'une ville" not to the buildings and material layout of the city but to the question of the poetic form appropriate to city life), is intended to signify that the new genre brought into being by the 1869 publication of *Le Spleen* in the apparently random conformation that it thus came to have, is a writerly form—an *écriture*—devoted to the representation of the noisiness of time and change as an atmospherics of the city. "La forme d'une ville" denies subjective agency in favor of a collective experience of temporality.

In a letter to Sainte-Beuve, Baudelaire characterized the unstructured form of the collection he had still, in 1866, not managed to unify, as that of a leisurely stroll or flânerie, one that he thought reminiscent of Sainte-Beuve's own (verse) collection of 1829, *Vie, Poésies et Pensées de Joseph Delorme*:

> j'ai l'espoir de pouvoir montrer, un de ces jours, un nouveau Joseph Delorme accrochant sa pensée rhapsodique à chaque accident de sa flânerie et tirant de chaque objet une morale désagréable.
>
> (I hope to be able, one of these days, to show a new Joseph Delorme attaching his rhapsodic thought to every random happenstance of his stroll and drawing from each object of his attention an unpleasant moral.)
>
> (*C* 2:583)

But this characterization excludes, for example, the allegorical fables in *Le Spleen*, and the prose poem versions of verse lyrics, emphasizing only the texts that correspond to a poetics of everyday encounter. So rather than a flânerie structure, I want to propose in what follows that the readerly experience the collection mediates by its diary- or workbook-like structure is closer to the preteritional sense of time's passing that is enacted in "À une passante" or even "Le Cygne." Or rather, to an eventless version of that experience, one characteristic not of history but of the everyday, as "what is happening when nothing is happening." This is time as the ongoing interchange of future becoming past and past becoming future, in which something is always being constructed and something always being destroyed, the so-called present being indistinguishable from this ordinarily unperceived process of perpetual entropic-negentropic flux.

A more compelling model than flânerie for the supposed present, understood as a noisy site of temporality, would be that of the *chantier* or construction site, so familiar to Parisians in the age of Haussmann. A construction site is by definition also a demolition site; and the messy *chantier* of the quartier du Doyenné that is so closely connected, in "Le Cygne," to the poet's memory of the suffering swan and what it signifies is consequently a model for the readerly experience of time and noise—the permanent but perpetually changing interaction of entropy and negentropy—that is mediated by the diary-like, now-this-now-that form of *Le Spleen* as it has reached us. I mean that the concept of work in progress has become generic here, in the form of the collection; and that in so doing it likewise comes to constitute the *form* of the city. For work in progress, as Baudelaire puts it, is a snake that has no head or tail because it simply continues, either all head or all tail (or both). And thus there is in fact no progress at all, just time that passes, as Baudelaire understands it, in the endless losing battle of human negentropy against the force of entropy, the threat of noise, the sign of the Enemy: more a "travail en cours" (ongoing work) than work in progress, and as much travail (in the sense of the English word) as it is actual work.

In French, the word *chantier* is proverbial for disorder and mess; but Baudelaire associates it also with the passing of time, on the one hand, and the concomitant action of memory on the other. "Le Cygne" carefully traces the time layering associated with the sighting of the swan, the *feuilleté* effect of a history that moves relentlessly forward, from the now disappeared "vieux Paris" of which the Doyenné was once a part, through the remembered construction site associated with the stranded bird, to the time of the "nouveau Carrousel" that the narrator is crossing at his moment of epiphany, when the thought of Andromache provides the allegorical key to the puzzle of the swan's significance. These different ways of referring to the same patch of ground rehearse the changes it undergoes in passing through time, while the inevitability of such passing is played out at the start, in the switch from the present tense of the exclamation: "Andromaque, je pense à vous!" to the immediately following past tense of an explanatory narrative: "Ce petit fleuve . . . / A fécondé soudain ma mémoire fertile, / Comme je traversais le nouveau Carrousel." No sooner has the triumphant, time-denying exclamation occurred than it has already become part of a remembered past: the past that stretches back to the "vieux Paris" (and indeed to Andromache).

So even as memory works against time, time is relentlessly moving on: negentropy takes place, but it can occur only reactively, in the context of entropy, as the poem moves into its own long mulling-over, a moving-on that is also a failure to progress. It is this interaction of negentropy and entropy that makes the messiness of the construction site, as a site of work in progress that fails to progress, so emblematic of the noisiness of time, as it is exemplified by the poem's own endlessly backward-looking forward movement:

> Je ne vois qu'en esprit tout ce camp de baraques,
> Ces tas de chapiteaux ébauchés et de fûts,
> Les herbes, les gros blocs verdis par l'eau des flaques
> Et, brillant aux carreaux, le bric-à-brac confus.

And meanwhile the dawn racket of the street workers, associated with the awakening of "le Travail," adds further density to the temporal connotations of this messy, noisy site where work and antiwork meet and, as it were, join endless battle, a political allusion (to the June massacres) subtending the metaphysical reference to time's noisy flux.[5]

But if, as I am suggesting, *Le Spleen*, like "Le Cygne," has the generic character of a *chantier*, the site of endlessly ongoing work and antiwork that is constitutive of time also offers a model for understanding the character of Baudelaire's work as a whole, what is referred to as his *oeuvre*. Not so much an *oeuvre*—a word that implies completion—as it is a site where the construction of poetry takes the form of constant experimentation and change, and hence of instability and disorder rather than unity and orderly development, Baudelaire's work is best thought of as an (allegorical) monument, in its failure to cohere and its incompletion, to the historical experience it teaches us to call modernity. Full of elisions, gaps, incoherences, afterthoughts, changes of mind and allusiveness, it constitutes a fragmentary record, one that makes readable the time that was lived, preteritionally, by an observer of remarkable sensitivity, complexity, and astuteness, in the confusion and jumble, the "chaos mouvant" of the historical construction site, the ongoing *chantier*, that was the rapidly growing and changing city of Paris in the era of France's modernization.

To read such a record of constant change is in turn to be continually destabilized, "dépassé par l'événement," obliged to revise one's understanding. However, such a view of writing—as at one and the same time a historical detritus and an *agencement* or device designed to keep the reader in a permanently changing state of instability and uncertainty—is doubtless the modernizing achievement, and the art of disalienation, for which we ought to be most grateful to Baudelaire, who invented such writing as the form given by art to the city and its noisy atmosphere, that is to time. In that respect, *Le Spleen de Paris*, understood as a poet's urban diary that lacks head or tail because it is all head and all tail, is the very epitome of Baudelairean *poiesis,* as a work in progress that denies the possibility of progress; but also of the body of his writing understood as a *Nachlass,* unfinished and unfinishable—more an energy than an *ergon.* Something left behind, abandoned—but also given over. Something left *for us,* to "make" of it what we can.

Baudelaire's natural death, a consequence of time that makes *Le Spleen* a *Nachlass,* resonates strangely, then, with the metaphorical "death of the author" evidenced in the formlessness and unfinishedness that makes this heterogeneous collection readable, nevertheless, as a meaningful artistic intervention: one that gives the ever-changing city its form as a *chantier,* noisy with the work of time. What we are to make of what has been left to us—time's *Nachlass*—is very much a matter, in other words, of the generic options available to us, and of the assumptions they entail. And it is on that understanding that I propose the following hypothesis: a suitable reading frame for *Le Spleen*—and by extension for the *chantier*-like *oeuvre,* or rather *energeia,* of which it is a fragment—is that of a certain kind of diary. A poet's diary certainly, as I have said. But a poet's diary that, to the extent that it constitutes a diary of urban existence, reads as a record of the so-called death of the author that is a consequence of the authorial subject's own subordination to the erosion of time, the work of the city.

As I pointed out in chapter 5, Baudelaire's poems of urban *croisement* differ from flâneur writing by virtue of the critical character of their analysis of alienated city life; as he wrote to Sainte-Beuve, he is a Joseph Delorme "tirant de chaque objet une morale désagréable" (*C* 2:583). Such texts also do not exhaust the wide range of different kinds of texts that make up the collection. But the tradition of flâneur writing is relevant to *Le Spleen de Paris* in one important way: as something like a *reportage* concerning the everyday it was, like news gathering in general, a collective enterprise in which individual authorship—the individual pieces were, of course, signed—was ultimately secondary to a much more general project. As an investigation of the new way of life that had been formed in the emergent social organization accompanying the industrial revolution, flâneur journalism was a kind of collective *bricolage*. And as such it was piecemeal in its approach, widely diverse in its interpretations, evaluations and judgments, haphazard in its choice of reportable subject matter, and variable as to style and point of view.

If it attested to the becoming newsworthy of everyday life under the conditions of modernity, its project was perhaps never clearly defined: given that it aimed in a general way to introduce citizens to the way of life of neighbors with whom they might live cheek-by-jowl without having any form of insight into their conditions of existence, was this understood or understandable as a matter of information, of entertainment, of moral judgment, or political ideology? Was it merely *reportage* or did it constitute literature? And what was its relation to the other modes of writing that made up the *feuilleton* and together defined the category of the *feuilletonesque*, by contrast with the more consequent journalistic reporting that belonged "above the fold"?

Perhaps its character was best defined as anecdotal, a word whose etymological sense (not previously given out, or edited) cagily fails to specify what it might be in the *inédit* that is of positive value, beyond its novelty. In that capacity, it constitutes a likely generic candidate for an atmospherics of the city, given its proclivity for a function that might be described as making the previously unnoticed noteworthy. And the collective character of its reporting, the jumble of its reports and the noisiness of their informational content, make it a site of nearly anonymous writing in which the so-called death of the author is, if not definitively enacted, clearly foreshadowed. Anecdotes circulate freely, without its being necessary to specify either their source, or the point they are taken to make, let alone the actual significance that point might have. However, if flâneur writing suggests in this way a relation between a writing that makes readable, as its unstated collective point, the otherwise subliminal atmosphere generated by city life and the concomitant death of the author, its suggestivity as a forerunner or prototype of *Le Spleen de Paris* has nothing of the precision with which Baudelaire's writing permits us to identify the noise of time as the object of an atmospherics whose writing entails the disappearance of authorial subjectivity. So I will briefly turn to a more recent manifestation of the flâneur project.

The figure of the flâneur is, of course, no longer a familiar sight in city streets. However, the function subserved by flâneur writing remains sufficiently relevant that variants of flâneur practice survive in contemporary journalism. One such variant is what the *New York Times* calls its "metropolitan diary," of which versions exist in many daily newspapers. Ordinary citizens leading presumably busy lives are invited to contribute very short pieces—occasionally poems, but ordinarily prose, and typically anecdotal in character—concerning incidents they may have observed or been involved in, in the course of their daily life in the city. Each week, the *Times* publishes an apparently random group of such contributions, usually with an illustration provided by a staff artist, the unstated implication being that such a collection of unrelated accounts provides more or better insight into what it is like to be a citizen of New York than, say, the work of a specifically assigned professional reporter. That is, such incidents, taken individually but also severally, are held to be simultaneously *characteristic* of "life in this city" and *unusual* enough, in their very typicality, to be striking and worthy of attention, that is, reportable. Their value lies in their being, paradoxically, even more characteristic in their rarity and particularity than are the vast majority of other anonymous encounters, transactions and *croisements* that occur daily, it being perhaps unnecessary to add that in this respect their *point* is, however, never spelled out, being allowed to emerge as a function of their relation to the other, similarly inexplicit anecdotes in whose company they appear.

The project amounts in this way to an exercise that produces noisiness—that implicit in the individual encounters as well as that arising from their collection—as implicitly meaningful. That contributors, at least, often have in mind an atmospherics of the city as an exploration of its local color is indicated, furthermore, by the frequency with which they refer, explicitly or implicitly, to prevailing myths that define the city in question. Acts of random kindness are reportable because they belie the myth of New York as an urban jungle. The "Arbor Anecdotes" sometimes published in the undergraduate newspaper of the University of Michigan, to take another example of the genre, tend to endorse overwhelmingly the myth of Ann Arbor that has prevailed since the 1960s—contrary to all evidence—as a city of bohemians, eccentrics, and weirdos. Either way, a city is defined by its atmospherics, understood as that product of its collective life and history that can be signified but not stated, and thus as the object of a task of exemplification perpetually *en cours*.

If no common thread is detectable in the items published in a given week, there is also, of course, no cohesion, no thematic or other thread, in the selections that appear week by week. The "Metropolitan Diary" has been a fixture of the *Times* for many years; one wonders how many readers recall last week's edition in reading this week's, or look for ways in which it may anticipate the content of the following week's as the series extends through time and imitates, in its own way, not only time's headless-and-tailless, all-head-and-all-tail continuity, but also the noisy, *chantier*-like properties of each successive moment, as time passes and passes us by. The genre of the metropolitan diary, then, is one that locates the city's atmospheric character as a matter of readability substituting for communicability, while simultaneously identifying time as a phenomenon of change and changeability that resists stabilization through becoming known. To conflate the epistemological unavailability of the latter with the readability—which is also to say the unreadability—that characterizes the former is the function of the metropolitan diary as a genre devoted to a poetics of noise.

Le Spleen de Paris is manifestly not collectively written, and its heterogeneity derives from the versatility of the prose poem form that Baudelaire was exploring and, in part, inventing. This versatility encompasses the ironic anecdote of urban encounter (what one of the poet's own attempts at classification called "choses parisiennes"), the "disfiguring" of lyrics in verse (as identified by Barbara Johnson), dream poems ("onéirocritie"), allegorical fables ("symboles et moralités"), and other possibilities still, including those that are suggested by the lists of ideas for future titles that Baudelaire left behind at his death.[6] Taken together with the difficulty one has in detecting any principle of thematic coherence governing the order in which the poems appear, such a variety of functions strongly suggests the idea that the collection amounts to something like a poet's workbook, constituting as it were a *personal* metropolitan diary, a blog dating from the era of paper, pen, and printing press. Without recognizable introduction (although "L'Étranger" is a striking characterization of the poet subject's own alienated position of observation), and without a conclusive ending, *Le Spleen* reads equally well as a sort of poetic *chantier*, and as a poet observer's record of time passed, one in which what becomes readable is the same secret Enemy to which, as a writing of time, the journalistic genre I am comparing it to lends itself.

However, its frequent irony, acerbic tone, and *moralités désagréables* also give it the tone of a critical *dossier,* accumulating in time like that of a *juge d'instruction* putting together materials for an indictment and a trial. There is a unity of critical intention and indeed of judgment here that is alien to the journalistic metropolitan diary and indeed to flâneur writing in general, more devoted to reporting than to issues of *process* (a word that refers both to temporal flow and to constructing a case, as in French *procès,* so that it is as if time, once detected, became the agent of its own critique). And it is in this that the prose poem collection, as a genre simulating time's passing while cultivating the critical detachment of an observing bystander, conforms to an idea of "modern beauty" as an aesthetics of disalienation, the idea whose evolution we have been witnessing in this essay. We are plunged into the very sensation, or *aisthesis,* of time's preteritional passing by while simultaneously finding ourselves *dépassés*—left behind and baffled, estranged and puzzled. This making sensible of process is a way to *faire le procès* of time the Enemy; and an aesthetics of noise is the agent that simultaneously *makes time sensible* and, by its interference in the reading *process,* brings about the *distancing effect* of its unreadability—the effect, that is, that enforces judgment.

Modern beauty, then, is an atmospherics of the city in just this sense. But the atmospherics of *Le Spleen* is like the window casually thrown open onto the noisy city by the narrator figure of "Le mauvais vitrier" in that it is itself—wonderfully—an unforeseen consequence, the incontrovertible and irreversible outcome of an accident; that is, of noise. The death of the author—his real death certainly, but also the metaphorical death that is loss of control over a developing, would-be *oeuvre*—proves to have been the necessary agency responsible for the emergence not only of a new genre but, more generally, also of new understandings of art's defining alliance, in modernity, with the power of noise.

"Chassez le naturel, il revient au galop." Boileau's maxim—"Get rid of the natural, back it comes at full speed"—has become proverbial because it describes a dynamics that Freud identified, in due course, as the return of the repressed. With respect to the repression of noise, the same dynamics describes the evolution I have traced here in Baudelaire, from an illusionist poetics of fetishizing "magic" attributed to the power of form—form, that is, as antinoise—to an *aisthesis* of temporality, in which the noise of perpetual change itself becomes "la forme d'une ville." Time denied, along with the disorder that is the sign of its destructive power, comes galloping back, albeit transformed—as Freud would have predicted—into a supernaturalism of history, a version of the uncanny. What the *Salon de 1846* described as *le merveilleux* becomes a metaphysics of *le mal*, and poetry in turn becomes no longer an instrument of comfortable illusion, but a detector of secret presence, and an agent of disalienation in the form of "la conscience dans le Mal."

Following the work of Elizabeth Cardonne-Arlyck, one might wish to identify such an evolution in Baudelaire as the invention of a poetics of veracity, where "veracity" names modern poetry's ethical struggle to recognize, acknowledge, and assume into its own work of *poiesis* that which is definitionally alien to it: in Baudelaire's case the city, where time reigns and is manifested as noise.[7] *Atmospherics* is the name I have given in this book to such a poetics of veracity, evolving, as it does in Baudelaire, from the aura that surrounds objects illusorily released by fetish aesthetics from the laws of time. For Baudelaire is, in fact, not the poet conceived by Boileau, reconciling the demands of artifice with those of the natural so as to produce an art of classic balance and grace. And this is because the category of the natural is inaccessible to him, understood as it is as a space of timelessness, but one whose law has been infringed by human history, following a mythic fall identified with the creation of urban civilization and beginning with Troy. And mankind, as a consequence, is condemned, in Baudelaire's vision, to the evil of artifice, while time—less a manifestation of the natural than evidence of the real—becomes the alien other: that which punishes both humans themselves, and their artificial creations, the agency of *le Mal*.

The fetishistic aura that arises from the denial of time is no less a sign of the urban, therefore, than is the "atmospherics" that makes readable time's evil presence. Both the denial of time, as a flight into illusion, and its recognition, as an act of disalienation, are evidence of an original, and thus irredeemable fall: the eponymous "irrémédiable" of the poem that describes, as our only acceptable option, "la conscience dans le Mal."

Closer ancestors to Baudelaire than Boileau would therefore be figures like Wordsworth, already conscious of the nature/city split, and Hölderlin, already engaged in an ethical poetics—a "poéthique"—of noise (in its German Romantic guise as "permanent digression" or the "alternation of tones"). And because Baudelaire's inheritors are in turn the nontranscendentalist, sublimity-deprived poets of the latter part of the twentieth century—the veracious exponents, in Elisabeth Cardonne-Arlyck's analysis, of a poetics of time (Ponge, Jaccottet, Roubaud, Deguy)—I would venture to count him, like Marx or Freud, among those whom Michel Foucault described as modern founders of discourse, or "fondateurs de discursivité."[8] He is the inaugurator of *la beauté moderne* as an ethics of aesthetic practice that entails permanent unfinishedness.

For by now it is surely a norm, not solely of poetry but of art in general, that it takes nonart, or rather antiart—and thus inevitably some manifestation of entropy—as the challenging other that it must assimilate, assume, and above all, frame (that is, make available) for reactions of awe, contemplation, curiosity, anger, fear, rejection, dejection, or, in short, for reading. It is in that way and for that reason that Baudelaire's *Nachlass* has become a legacy, precisely to the extent that it failed ever to become an *oeuvre*.

So it is as if the *chantier* that Baudelaire set up continues to operate, as a "travail en cours," in the efforts of his successors, who in turn transmit it, a still unaccomplished task, to Rimbaud's "d'autres horribles travailleurs." All are engaged in a vast collective effort: the struggle, to have recourse once more to Rimbaud, to *trouver une langue*, that is, to invent the writerly idiom, discover the genre, devise the atmospherics best suited to bespeak the terrifying power, as well as the intense fascination, exerted by poetry's implacable and indomitable *other*, which I have called noise.[9] The veracity of modern art, its manner of bearing witness, turns out in this way to entail, not an achievement but an endless, because never fully resolved, pursuit of the veracious.

"Le Cygne"—homologous with that collective pattern in its own representation of an endless, unresolved personal mulling over or *penser à*— authorizes us to identify this dynamic of the inconclusive as melancholic: melancholic because conscious of its modernity, and modern because afflicted with melancholy. For to be melancholic is to be conscious of history, as a story of loss and the sign of humanity's fallen state: to recognize it, that is, hanging like a pall over the city. It is to be conscious of one's alienation, then, but also and for that reason to be in a position to *bear witness*, to testify to that sense of estrangement and loss—and in doing so to bring to others the sad grace of disalienation, "la conscience dans le Mal." The price to pay for this privilege of the testimonial is the endless pursuit of veracity. Nevertheless therein lies, for Baudelaire and his successors, the only dignity to which, in modernity, the practice of poetry, with its own long history, can aspire.

APPENDIX

Le Cygne

I

Andromaque, je pense à vous! Ce petit fleuve,
Pauvre et triste miroir où jadis resplendit
L'immense majesté de vos douleurs de veuve,
Ce Simoïs menteur qui par vos pleurs grandit,

A fécondé soudain ma mémoire fertile,
Comme je traversais le nouveau Carrousel.
Le vieux Paris n'est plus (la forme d'une ville
Change plus vite, hélas! que le cœur d'un mortel);

Je ne vois qu'en esprit tout ce camp de baraques,
Ces tas de chapiteaux ébauchés et de fûts,
Les herbes, les gros blocs verdis par l'eau des flaques,
Et, brillant aux carreaux, le bric-à-brac confus.

Là s'étalait jadis une ménagerie;
Là je vis, un matin, à l'heure où sous les cieux
Froids et clairs le Travail s'éveille, où la voirie
Pousse un sombre ouragan dans l'air silencieux,

Un cygne qui s'était évadé de sa cage,
Et, de ses pieds palmés frottant le pavé sec,
Sur le sol raboteux traînait son blanc plumage.
Près d'un ruisseau sans eau la bête ouvrant le bec

Baignait nerveusement ses ailes dans la poudre,
Et disait, le cœur plein de son beau lac natal:
«Eau, quand donc pleuvras-tu? quand tonneras-tu, foudre?»
Je vois ce malheureux, mythe étrange et fatal,

Vers le ciel quelquefois, comme l'homme d'Ovide,
Vers le ciel ironique et cruellement bleu,
Sur son cou convulsif tendant sa tête avide,
Comme s'il adressait des reproches à Dieu!

II

Paris change! mais rien dans ma mélancolie
N'a bougé! palais neufs, échafaudages, blocs,
Vieux faubourgs, tout pour moi devient allégorie,
Et mes chers souvenirs sont plus lourds que des rocs.

Aussi devant ce Louvre une image m'opprime:
Je pense à mon grand cygne, avec ses gestes fous,
Comme les exilés, ridicule et sublime,
Et rongé d'un désir sans trêve! et puis à vous,

Andromaque, des bras d'un grand époux tombée,
Vil bétail, sous la main du superbe Pyrrhus,
Auprès d'un tombeau vide en extase courbée;
Veuve d'Hector, hélas! et femme d'Hélénus!

Je pense à la négresse, amaigrie et phtisique,
Piétinant dans la boue, et cherchant, l'œil hagard,
Les cocotiers absents de la superbe Afrique
Derrière la muraille immense du brouillard;

À quiconque a perdu ce qui ne se retrouve
Jamais, jamais! à ceux qui s'abreuvent de pleurs

Et tètent la Douleur comme une bonne louve!
Aux maigres orphelins séchant comme des fleurs!

Ainsi dans la forêt où mon esprit s'exile
Un vieux Souvenir sonne à plein souffle du cor!
Je pense aux matelots oubliés dans une île,
Aux captifs, aux vaincus! . . . à bien d'autres encor!

The Swan

I

Andromache, I think of you! That stream,
the sometime witness to your widowhood's
enormous majesty of mourning—that
mimic Simoïs salted by your tears

suddenly inundates my memory
as I cross the new Place du Carrousel.
Old Paris is gone (no human heart
changes half so fast as a city's face)

and only in my mind's eye can I see
the junk laid out to glitter in the booths
among the weeds and splintered capitals,
blocks of marble blackened by the mud;

there used to be a poultry-market here,
and one cold morning—with the sky swept clean,
the ground, too, swept by garbage-men who raised
clouds of soot in the icy air—I saw

a swan that had broken out of its cage,
webbed feet clumsy on the cobblestones,
white feathers dragging in the uneven ruts,
and obstinately pecking at the drains,

drenching its enormous wings in the filth
as if in its own lovely lake, crying
"Where is the thunder, when will it rain?"
I see it still, inevitable myth,

like Daedalus dead-set against the sky—
the sky quite blue and blank and unconcerned—
that straining neck and that voracious beak,
as if the swan were castigating God!

2

Paris changes . . . But in sadness like mine
nothing stirs—new buildings, old
neighborhoods turn to allegory,
and memories weigh more than stone.

One image, near the Louvre, will not dissolve:
I think of that great swan in its torment,
silly, like all exiles, and sublime,
endlessly longing . . . And again I think

of you, Andromache, dragged off
to be the booty of Achilles's son,
Hector's widow now the wife of Helenus,
crouching blindly over an empty grave!

I think of some black woman, starving
and consumptive in the muddy streets,
peering through a wall of fog for those
missing palms of splendid Africa;

I think of orphans withering like flowers;
of those who lose what never can be found
again—never! swallowing their tears
and nursing at the she-wolf Sorrow's dugs;

and in the forest of my mind's exile
a merciless memory winds its horn:
I hear it and I think of prisoners,
of the shipwrecked, the beaten—and so many more!

Les sept vieillards

Fourmillante cité, cité pleine de rêves,
Où le spectre en plein jour raccroche le passant!
Les mystères partout coulent comme des sèves
Dans les canaux étroits du colosse puissant.

Un matin, cependant que dans la triste rue
Les maisons, dont la brume allongeait la hauteur,
Simulaient les deux quais d'une rivière accrue,
Et que, décor semblable à l'âme de l'acteur,

Un brouillard sale et jaune inondait tout l'espace,
Je suivais, roidissant mes nerfs comme un héros
Et discutant avec mon âme déjà lasse,
Le faubourg secoué par les lourds tombereaux.

Tout à coup, un vieillard dont les guenilles jaunes
Imitaient la couleur de ce ciel pluvieux,
Et dont l'aspect aurait fait pleuvoir les aumônes,
Sans la méchanceté qui luisait dans ses yeux,

M'apparut. On eût dit sa prunelle trempée
Dans le fiel; son regard aiguisait les frimas,
Et sa barbe à longs poils, roide comme une épée,
Se projetait, pareille à celle de Judas.

Il n'était pas voûté, mais cassé, son échine
Faisant avec sa jambe un parfait angle droit,
Si bien que son bâton, parachevant sa mine,
Lui donnait la tournure et le pas maladroit

D'un quadrupède infirme ou d'un juif à trois pattes.
Dans la neige et la boue il allait s'empêtrant,
Comme s'il écrasait des morts sous ses savates,
Hostile à l'univers plutôt qu'indifférent.

Son pareil le suivait: barbe, œil, dos, bâton, loques,
Nul trait ne distinguait, du même enfer venu,
Ce jumeau centenaire, et ces spectres baroques
Marchaient du même pas vers un but inconnu.

À quel complot infâme étais-je donc en butte,
Ou quel méchant hasard ainsi m'humiliait?
Car je comptai sept fois, de minute en minute,
Ce sinistre vieillard qui se multipliait!

Que celui-là qui rit de mon inquiétude,
Et qui n'est pas saisi d'un frisson fraternel,
Songe bien que malgré tant de décrépitude
Ces sept monstres hideux avaient l'air éternel!

Aurais-je, sans mourir, contemplé le huitième,
Sosie inexorable, ironique et fatal,
Dégoûtant Phénix, fils et père de lui-même?
—Mais je tournai le dos au cortège infernal.

Exaspéré comme un ivrogne qui voit double,
Je rentrai, je fermai ma porte, épouvanté,
Malade et morfondu, l'esprit fiévreux et trouble,
Blessé par le mystère et par l'absurdité!

Vainement ma raison voulait prendre la barre;
La tempête en jouant déroutait ses efforts,
Et mon âme dansait, dansait, vieille gabarre
Sans mâts, sur une mer monstrueuse et sans bords!

The Seven Old Men

Swarming city—city gorged with dreams,
where ghosts by day accost the passer-by,
where secrets run in these defiled canals
like blood that gushes through a giant's veins!

One morning when the rain in these mean streets
made houses grimmer than the docks that line
the two banks of a filthy river, and
a yellow fog engulfed the space between—

a stage-effect to match the actor's mood—
I roamed as if in search of stern resolve
and arguments to steel my flagging soul
through backstreets shaken by each heavy van.

And out of nowhere came a wretch in rags
the very color of the dripping sky—
surely *this* deserved some charity!
But then I saw the malice in his eyes

and seemed to feel the cold because of them—
as if their pupils had been soaked in bile.
His beard stuck out as stiff as any sword
(Judas must have had a beard like that).

He wasn't bent, he was *broken,* and his spine
formed so sharp an angle with his legs
that his stick, as if to add a finishing touch,
gave him the carriage and the clumsy gait

of some lame animal or a three-legged Jew!
He pounded past in the mud and slush as if
his shabby boots were crushing dead men's bones—
hostile, rather than indifferent . . .

Then from the same hell came another, the same
eyes and beard and backbone, stick and rags—
nothing distinguished these centenarian twins
clumping identically toward an unknown goal.

Was it some vile conspiracy, or just
coincidence that made a fool of me?
To the seventh power—I counted every one—
this sinister ancient reproduced himself!

Doubtless to you my dread seems ludicrous,
unless a brotherly shudder lets you see:
for all their imminent decrepitude,
these seven monsters had eternal life!

I doubt it I could have survived an eighth
such apparition, father and son of himself,
inexorable Phoenix, loathsome avatar!
—I turned my back on the whole damned parade.

Indignant as a drunk who sees the world
double, I staggered home and locked my door,
scared and sick at heart and scandalized
that so much mystery could be absurd!

Vainly my reason sought to take the helm—
the gale made light of purpose, and my soul
went dancing on, an old and mastless scow
dancing across a black and shoreless sea.

NOTES

1. FROM THE SUBLIME TO THE SUBLIMINAL: FETISH AESTHETICS

1. Etymologically, allegory (Greek *allo+gorein,* to speak) means speaking other(wise).

2. "Chaos mouvant" is quoted from "Perte d'auréole" (*Le Spleen de Paris,* poem 46).

3. Antianaesthetics as disalienation rephrases Claire Lyu's understanding of what she calls Baudelaire's "antinarcotic" project, an idea she derives from a careful reading of *Les Paradis artificiels* (1860). See Claire Chi-ah Lyu, *A Sun Within a Sun. The Power and the Elegance of Poetry* (Pittsburgh, PA: University of Pittsburgh Press, 2006).

4. *Fétiche* was imported into French, via Portuguese *feitiço* (fabricated object) to designate the ceremonial figures brought back to Europe from West Africa by traders; and it retains that sense throughout the greater part of the nineteenth century, although Rétif de la Bretonne had identified his own foot fetishism as such at the turn of the century. See Amy Wyngard, "The Fetish in/as Text: Rétif de la Bretonne and the Development of Modern Sexual Science and French Literary Studies," *PMLA* 121, no. 3 (May 2006): 662–86. Marx famously identified commodity fetishism in *Das Kapital* (1867); but "fetish aesthetics" is my own coinage to designate the idealizing aesthetics common to the generation of Gautier, Nerval, Flaubert, and Baudelaire, and often imagined by them in the framework of a country-city contrast (cf. Nerval's "Sylvie" and

Flaubert's *Madame Bovary*). For expanded discussions of fetish aesthetics, see my "On Inventing Unknownness: the Poetry of Disenchanted Reenchantment," *French Forum* 33, nos. 1–2 (2008): 15–36, and "Modern Beauty: Baudelaire, the Everyday, Cultural Studies," *Romance Studies* 26, no. 3 (July 2008): 249–70.

5. See M. H. Abrams, *Natural Supernaturalism* (London: Oxford University Press, 1971).

6. On shamanism as a practice of "skilled revelation of skilled deception" producing such a form of transparency, see Michael Taussig, "Viscerality, Faith and Skepticism. Another Theory of Magic," in *Walter Benjamin's Grave* (Chicago: University of Chicago Press, 2006).

7. David Harvey's *Paris Capital of Modernity* (London and New York: Routledge, 2006) reproduces a number of striking images of the various forms of disruption introduced into the lives of Parisians by the city's modernization.

8. See in particular Patrick Greaney, *Untimely Beggar. Poverty and Power from Baudelaire to Benjamin* (Minneapolis: University of Minnesota Press, 2008), esp. chap. 2. David Harvey in *Paris Capital of Modernity* offers a careful discussion of the lives of the Parisian working class during this period which omits all reference to the street people or *forains*. (He does reproduce a well-known Daumier representing street musicians.) I take this as an indicator of the marginality of lives that escaped the attention of the contemporary surveys and the other accounts on which Harvey draws.

9. Gail Jones, *Dreams of Speaking* (Sydney: Random House, 2006).

10. See my discussion in chapters 3 and 4 of "Le Cygne," "Les sept vieillards," and "À une passante."

11. Baudelaire remained interested in Gautier as a poet, despite his own new aesthetic (and political) orientation. "Les sept vieillards," for example, owes something of its atmosphere—as well as some verbal echoes ("spectre(s) en plein jour")—to Gautier's very Bonapartist "Vieux de la Vieille. 15 Décembre" (in *Emaux et Camées*).

12. See Walter Benjamin, *The Origin of the German Tragic Drama* (London: Verso, 1975), "Allegory and Trauerspiel," 159–235. (*Ursprung des deutschen Trauerspiels* [Frankfurt am Main: Suhrkamp, 1963]).

13. See *Mon coeur mis à nu*, X (OC 1:682): "Ce que j'ai toujours trouvé de plus beau dans un théâtre, dans mon enfance, et encore maintenant, c'est le lustre—un bel objet lumineux, cristallin, compliqué, circulaire

et symétrique." (What I've always thought most beautiful in the theater, both in my childhood and still now, is the chandelier—an object beautiful, luminous, crystalline, complex, circular and symmetrical.)

14. Such a strategic outbreak of disorder may well be the 4-4-3-2 stanzaic structure of "Les sept vieillards," which suggests a lame or deformed sonnet. See my article "Daylight Specter," *Yale French Studies* nos. 125–26 (2014): 45–65.

2. THE MAGIC WINDOWPANE

1. See Amy Wyngard, "The Fetish in/as Text: Rétif de la Bretonne and the Development of Modern Sexual Science and French Literary Studies, 1887–1934," *PMLA* 121, no. 3 (May 2006): 662–86. This article traces the prehistory of the Freudian (erotic) fetish.

2. Gérard de Nerval, "Sylvie," in *Œuvres*, vol. 1, éd. Albert Béguin and Jean Richer (Paris: Bibliothèque de la Pléiade, 1966), 247.

3. "Je n'ai pas oublié . . ." is poem 99 of the 1861 edition. Its actual date of composition is not known.

4. "Le mauvais vitrier" is poem 9 of *Le Spleen de Paris* (OC 1:285–87).

5. See Théophile Gautier, *Poésies complètes*, vol. 3, éd. René Jasinski (Paris: Nizet, 1970), 3. "Paysage" was first published in 1857. Its date of composition is unknown.

6. Gautier's "Préface" referred to the example of Goethe shutting himself away during the Napoleonic wars in order to write the *West-Östlicher Diwan* ("le *Divan occidental*,"line 3). On the significance of the storm in Baudelaire, see also "L'Ennemi" (poem 10) and "À une passante" (poem 93) discussed in chapters 3 and 4, respectively.

7. See "Le beau navire" (poem 52).

8. The fact that the sun is itself subject to entropy was, of course, not known to Baudelaire and his contemporaries.

9. I am thinking in particular of the striking representations of the boulevard de Sébastopol and the rue de Rennes reproduced in David Harvey, *Paris Capital of Modernity*, 262, fig. 91.

3. FETISHISM BECOMES ALLEGORY

1. Maurice Blanchot, "La parole quotidienne," in *L'Entretien infini* (Paris: Gallimard, 1969), 257.

2. "Time the anthropophagous / Swallows up each human work; / Christian, Muslim, Hindu, Turk, / Down his vast oesophagus, / Pass to their sarcophagus." (I do not know the provenance of this ditty.)

3. G. W. F. Hegel plays on these words in a famous comment from the preface to *The Phenomenology of Spirit* (para. 31) that M. H. Abrams adopted as an epigraph to *Natural Supernaturalism*: "Quite generally, the familiar (*bekannt*), just because it is familiar, is not cognitively understood (*erkannt*)."

4. Friedrich Schlegel, "Zur Philosophie" (1797), Fragment 668, in *Philosophische Lehrjahre I* (1796–1806), ed. Ernst Behler, *Kritische Friedrich Schlegel Ausgabe* (München: F. Schöning, 1958), 18:85.

5. Benjamin, *German Tragic Drama*, 178.

6. Metrically, "montrant sa jambe de statue" was possible, so it is being pointedly avoided in "A une passante." Notice, too, that as a rhyme word, *statue* recalls the noisy "Vénus" / "nus" rhyme of "Je n'ai pas oublié . . . ," with the further complication that, as a "feminine" rhyme, "statue" would normally be unavailable to rhyme with "Vénus" and "nus." However, in "À une dame créole" (poem 61), Baudelaire subverts the rule of alternating rhymes by alternating feminine rhymes ("gloire" / "Loire") with masculine rhymes ("manoirs" / "noirs") that have identical vowels, so he would have been sensitive to the way the "statue" / "tue" rhyme of "À une passante" reenacts the noisy "Vénus" / "nus" rhyme of "Je n'ai pas oublié . . . ."

7. See "Pourquoi la sculpture est ennuyeuse" (OC 2:487–89) and "Sculpture" (OC 2:669–80). Although "ennuyeuse" is normally understood to mean boring, I will be suggesting that, more or less latent, in the 1846 Salon, it is the secondary sense of *inconvenient, disturbing,* or *troublesome* that emerges in the 1859 essay. Similarly allegory can be regarded as a boringly ancient figure that, in Baudelaire's hands, becomes a signifier of modern anxiety.

8. On the nineteenth-century history of the word *fétiche,* see Amy Wyngard, "The Fetish in/as Text." The sense "ugly figure of primitive worship" was the only current one at mid-century. To my knowledge, this is the only occurrence of the word in Baudelaire.

9. See Sigmund Freud, "The Uncanny" ("Das Unheimliche"), 1919, in *The Uncanny*, trans. David McClintock (London: Penguin, 2003), 121–62. Etymologically, both English *haunt* and French *hanter* seem also to derive from the Germanic radical *haim* (cf. English *home* and French *hameau*).

10. Adjacent to the Cour du Louvre, Haussmann's Place du Carrousel became the site of a Napoleonic *arc de triomphe,* so that the site epitomizes the adjacency of the historically new and the historically old that is thematic in the poem. Before becoming a fairground entertainment, a carrousel was a space reserved for jousting (and later equestrian parades). Jousting resonates suggestively with the shock of encounter that, I will argue, is associated with the crossing point of chiasmic allegory.

11. Another hint of chiasmus occurs when, following the opening quatrain, part 2 reprises the narrational movement of part 1 (Andromaque-swan) but in reverse order: "je pense à mon grand cygne. . ." "et puis à vous, Andromaque. . .", before embarking, with the "négresse phtisique" of line 41, on the melancholic catalogue of instances of exile, loss, and abandonment that ends the poem on its inconclusive "à bien d'autres encor." If part 1 is to part 2 as allegory to melancholy, the latter re-echoes that movement in the relation of its own three opening stanzas to the final three, with the poignant picture of the negress, shuffling in the mud like the swan in the dust, corresponding at the center point to the evocation in part 1 of "l'éveil du Travail," the noisy street and the cold, clear heavens.

12. For a brilliant recent reading of "Le Cygne" as allegorical in a sense derived from Walter Benjamin's reflection on modernity (notably in the *Passagen-Werk*), see Kevin Newmark, "Who Needs Poetry? Baudelaire, Benjamin and the Modernity of 'Le Cygne,'" *Comparative Literature* 63, no. 3 (2011): 269–90.

4. DAYLIGHT SPECTERS: ALLEGORY AND THE WEATHER OF TIME

1. *Poésies complètes de Théophile Gautier,* 46–49.

2. See the appendix for the complete text and translation of "Les sept vieillards."

3. On Baudelairean double vision, see Françoise Meltzer, *Seeing Double: Baudelaire's Modernity* (Chicago: University of Chicago Press, 2011).

4. "Bare life" is Giorgio Agamben's term for the residual character of what survives the loss of self in the "vast experiment," as Primo Levi termed it, that was mounted in the Nazi extermination camps. See Agamben, *Homo Sacer: Sovereign Power and Bare Life* (Stanford, CA: Stanford University Press 1998).

5. The origin of the theory of the aesthetic impact of modern beauty as "coup de foudre" lay perhaps in the understanding of color harmony as the atmospherics of painting that a younger Baudelaire had developed in the *Salon de 1846* ("De la couleur"). "La bonne manière de savoir si un tableau est mélodieux est de le regarder d'assez loin pour n'en comprendre ni le sujet ni les lignes" (OC 2:425; the right way to discover whether a painting is melodic is to look at it from far enough away that neither its lines nor its subject can be discerned). Seen from a distance, the "passante" is a vision of harmony such as Baudelaire had believed in at that earlier time: as she moves closer, however, she also reveals her allegorical impact as that of the hurricane it harbors, along with insight into the power of the aesthetic as "la douceur qui fascine et le plaisir qui tue"?

6. Léon-Paul Fargue, *Haute solitude* (Paris: L'imaginaire, 1941), 59. Cited in Gilles Philippe and Julien Piat, eds., *La langue littéraire. Une histoire de la prose en France de Gustave Flaubert à Claude Simon* (Paris: Fayard, 2009), 269.

5. IRONIC ENCOUNTER: THE POETICS OF ANONYMITY

1. "L'Albatros" is poem 2 of *Les Fleurs du Mal.*

2. Cf. Baudelaire's letter to his mother of January 11, 1858: "J'ai laissé ces pièces sans titre et sans indications claires parce que j'ai horreur de prostituer les choses intimes de famille" (I left these poems titleless and without clear reference because I hate to prostitute intimate family matters) (C 1:445). The poems mentioned in my sentence are, in order of mention, poems 88, 91, 92, 100. "À une passante" (poem 93) is obviously the poem to which the anonymity of the two participants, to each other as well as to the reader, is most crucial.

3. See the famous letters to Georges Izambard and Paul Demeny of May 13 and 15, 1871. The "lettres du Voyant" are a *locus classicus* of the post-Baudelairean aesthetic turn to a language of noise.

4. The letter's irony arises from the backhanded flattery of a figure on whom Baudelaire was dependent for patronage but whose establishment position, poetry, aesthetics, and politics could only be antipathetic to him. There is a parallel between the glazier attempting to sell his goods to the perverse and assumedly bourgeois narrator of "Le mauvais vitrier" and Baudelaire's own relation to Houssaye.

5. Cf. "De l'héroïsme de la vie moderne," section XVIII of the *Salon de 1846* (OC 2:493–96).

6. See especially Dolf Oehler, *Ein Höllensturz der alten Welt* (Frankfurt a/M: Suhrkamp, 1988), translated by Guy Petitdemange as *Le Spleen contre l'oubli. Juin 1868. Baudelaire, Flaubert, Heine, Herzen* (Paris: Eds. Payot et Rivages, 1996), esp. chap. 6, 309–34.

7. Baudelaire's contempt for the idea of progress—something like official doctrine under the Second Empire—is especially prominent in his writings on Edgar Allan Poe.

8. Sonya Stephens, *Baudelaire's Prose Poems: The Practice and Politics of Irony* (Oxford: Oxford University Press, 1999); Marie Maclean, *Narrative as Performance. The Baudelairean Experiment* (London and New York: Routledge, 1988). My understanding of the cruelty of irony is akin to, and partly derived from, Debarati Sanyal's presentation of literary irony as a form of counterviolence, in *The Violence of Modernity. Baudelaire, Irony and the Politics of Form* (Baltimore, MD: John Hopkins University Press, 2006).

9. The editors in fact followed the most recent of Baudelaire's projected plans, but by omitting the section titles made the plan invisible. See also chapter 6, note 3.

10. My understanding of genre, not as a kind of text but as the set of presuppositions governing kinds of interaction, derives from the pragmatics of genre developed in particular by Anne Freadman. See, for example, her essays "Anyone for Tennis?" "Untitled (On Genre)," and "Genre Again. Another Shot," in, respectively, *The Place of Genre in Learning: Current Debates* (Geelong, AU: Deakin University Press, 1987), 71–94, *Cultural Studies* 2, no. 1 (January 1988): 67–99, and *Southern Review* 23 (November 1990): 251–61.

6. "LA FORME D'UNE VILLE": THE URBAN DIARY

1. On attention to the everyday in France since Baudelaire, see especially Michael Sheringham, *Everyday Life. Theories and Practices from Surrealism to the Present* (Oxford: Oxford University Press, 2006).

2. Allegory makes noise the object of an interpretive practice; irony introduces noise into the communication channel by making the relation of the subject of utterance to the utterance equivocal.

3. The surviving evidence suggests that Baudelaire envisaged a volume of prose poems structured in the same manner as *Les Fleurs du*

Mal. But he was experiencing difficulty in determining suitable categories under which to group the poems. After his death, his editors (Asselineau and Banville) adopted an order of poems that corresponded to that given in the most recent of Baudelaire's various projects, but at the same time they suppressed Baudelaire's proposed category headings. The outcome is that neither a thematic coherence of the poems nor an ordering of the volume as a whole is apparent. Randolph Runyon has recently demonstrated that the poems of *Le Spleen* (as well as of both editions of *Les Fleurs du Mal*) are linked to their neighbors by techniques of mainly verbal anticipation and reminiscence, a concatenation that he compares interestingly with Baudelaire's description of Wagner's cultivation of musical flow. (The metaphor of "le fil du temps" also comes to mind.) See R. Runyon, *Intratextual Baudelaire. The Sequential Fabric of* Les Fleurs du Mal *and* Le Spleen de Paris (Columbus: Ohio State University Press, 2010).

4. See Roland Barthes, "La mort de l'auteur," in *Le Bruissement de la langue* (Paris: Seuil, 1984), 61–67.

5. Possibly also the original meaning of the word *carrousel* (a jousting ground) is in play?

6. Barbara Johnson, *Défigurations du langage poétique. La seconde révolution baudelairienne* (Paris: Flammarion, 1979). Baudelaire's own notes toward his projected volume of prose poems are reproduced in OC 1:365–71 ("Reliquat du 'Spleen de Paris'").

7. Elisabeth Cardonne-Arlyck, *Véracités. Ponge, Jaccottet, Roubaud, Deguy* (Paris: Belin, 2009).

8. Michel Foucault, "Qu'est-ce qu'un auteur?" in *Dits et écrits 1954–1988* (Paris: Gallimard, 1994), 1:789–821.

9. Both Rimbaud quotations are from his famous letter of May 15, 1871, to Paul Demeny (the so-called "lettre du Voyant"). See A. Rimbaud, *Oeuvres Complètes,* ed. Steve Murphy (Paris: Honoré Champion, 1999), 249–54.

INDEX

VERBAL ARTS :: STUDIES IN POETICS

SERIES EDITORS :: Lazar Fleishman and Haun Saussy

Kiene Brillenburg Wurth, *Between Page and Screen: Remaking Literature Through Cinema and Cyberspace*

Jacob Edmond, *A Common Strangeness: Contemporary Poetry, Cross-Cultural Encounter, Comparative Literature*

Christophe Wall-Romana, *Cinepoetry: Imaginary Cinemas in French Poetry*

Marc Shell, *Talking the Walk and Walking the Talk: A Rhetoric of Rhythm*

Ryan Netzley, *Lyric Apocalypse: Milton, Marvell, and the Nature of Events*

Ilya Kliger and Boris Maslov (eds.), *Persistent Forms: Explorations in Historical Poetics*. Foreword by Eric Hayot

Ross Chambers, *An Atmospherics of the City: Baudelaire and the Poetics of Noise*